By the Power of the Holy Spirit

David M. Howard

InterVarsity Press
Downers Grove
Illinois 60515

Third printing, July 1975
© 1973 by Inter-Varsity
Christian Fellowship of the
United States of America.

InterVarsity Press is the
book publishing division of
Inter-Varsity Christian
Fellowship, a student movement
active on campus at hundreds
of universities, colleges and
schools of nursing. For information
about local and regional activities,
write IVCF, 233 Langdon St.,
Madison, WI 53703.

All Scripture quotations, unless
indicated otherwise, are from
the Revised Standard Version of the
Bible, copyrighted 1946 and 1952
by the Division of Christian Education
of the National Council of the
Churches of Christ in the U.S.A.,
and are used by permission.

ISBN 0-87784-358-9
Library of Congress Catalog
Card Number: 73-83091

Printed in the United
States of America

DEDICATION
to
Victor, Gregorio, Calixto, Maria
and other Colombians
who taught me by their lives
what the fullness of the
Holy Spirit means

CONTENTS

PREFACE

The past few years have seen more drastic up-heavals and changes in the student world than any comparable period in recent history. The activism of the late sixties, the drug culture, the growth of interest in the occult, the swing to Eastern mysticism, the rise of Women's Lib, the concern for ecology, plus a dozen other trends, have all been documented and analyzed in every major periodical and in scores of books. In the midst of all this ferment, Christian students have shown a notable interest in one topic perhaps more than any other, namely, the doctrine of the Holy Spirit. The questions of who he is, what he does in the life of the believer and especially what gifts he gives to the church are being discussed with increasing concern.

In travels throughout every major region of the United States and several areas of Canada I have yet to find a group of students who have not brought up this topic as being of vital importance both to individuals and to the group. These questions come with more consistency than any others. As I have interacted with students, learning from them and sharing with them in the study of the Word of God, I have been refreshed again and again as this doctrine has been considered. The response of students to what God says in his Word about the Spirit and what he wants for them through the Spirit has been most encouraging. For me it has been a continuation of the learning experiences God gave me during nine years in Colombia under the Latin America Mission. There I saw the Spirit of God at work in remarkable ways and learned much from believers whose spontaneous faith and sensitivity to the Spirit of God were great examples to me.

My entire adult ministry has been related to the world mission outreach of the church. Much of what I have learned about the Holy Spirit and his gifts to the church has been in the context of world evangelism and missions. Therefore, in attempting to share my understanding of the teaching of God's Word on this topic, I have chosen to do so with special focus on the missionary outreach of the church.

This book is not an exhaustive study of the doc-

trine of the Holy Spirit. Numerous competent scholars have done this far more ably than I could hope to do. Rather it is an endeavor to show the relationship of the Holy Spirit and his gifts to the responsibilities of the church in world evangelism. I have tried to do this in a biblical framework with illustrations from contemporary life.

After an introductory chapter outlining in general the doctrine of the Holy Spirit, we shall look at two aspects of his relationship to the individual believer: the baptism of the Spirit and the fullness of the Spirit. Then we shall discuss his relationship to the church as a corporate body, studying the relationship of the Holy Spirit to the Great Commission, the outreach of the church, the body of Christ and the gifts he gives the church. Because of the peculiar nature of and special interest in the gift of tongues, this topic will be considered separately in chapters 8 through 10. Finally, we shall try to apply all of this to the individual reader in chapter 11 and conclude with an epilogue to show how the Spirit is still at work.

If God can use this book to help Christian students and other believers to a better understanding of the place of the Holy Spirit and his gifts in their lives, I shall be grateful.

1
"HE SHALL GLORIFY ME."

It was a warm spring evening. The invitation from several friends to take a walk and discuss some things about the Lord was attractive, so I accepted. It was my freshman year in college. The desire to delve more deeply into the things of God was growing. I was pliable and open to any help that others wanted to give to help me know God better.

We walked a mile or two out into open fields beyond town and sat down in the grass. Our conversation centered on the Holy Spirit. My friends obviously knew more about the Spirit than I did and were anxious to lead me into a deeper understanding. I was impressed. Their sincerity and love were evident. Their personal touch with God seemed very real. They spoke at length about the immediate leading of the Spirit in their lives, a concept which was new and exciting to me. They spoke of death to self, of rebuking Satan and of asking guidance from the Spirit for every detail of life. My longings for a closer walk with God increased.

The next day, Bill, another friend several years older than I, whom I loved and highly respected, took me aside and said, "Dave, I understand you were out for a walk last night with _____ (naming several of the group of the previous evening). I have a pretty good idea why they invited you. Would you mind if I share with you some observations? I think a lot of you, Dave, and would hate to see you led astray."

He then proceeded to open the Scriptures and explain in clear and decisive terms the work of the Holy Spirit in the life of the individual believer. He spoke with deep feeling as he warned of the dangers of some concepts that my friends had shared with me. He pointed out that much of what they said was true but was being carried to an extreme which made it warped truth. Everything he said seemed to be based on the Scriptures.

Now the confusion set in. My other friends had seemed so right in what they had said. They wanted me to join in a more intimate fellowship with their group and help provide some continuity and leadership for reaching others with the same teachings. Yet Bill was such a godly man. He seemed so firm and well-grounded in his understanding of the Word. His humble walk with God was a stimulus to all who knew him.

For the next few days I struggled inwardly and prayed much that God would reveal his truth to me. I dug into the Bible in a desire to understand its truths more fully. My uncertainty and restlessness soon began to encroach on my sleep. If my friends were right, I needed to follow them on into deeper areas. If Bill was right, I needed to avoid involvement in something which might lead me into great error.

One night, after tossing restlessly in bed for several hours, I rose, dressed and went out to walk the streets. Passing the home of the godly pastor of the church I attended, I decided to rouse him and share my struggles. He came downstairs in his bathrobe and invited me into the parlor. He listened patiently as I told him the story.

Then he quietly opened the Bible and began to respond to my doubts and confusion. He spoke gently of my friends, expressing an understanding of their viewpoint, but showed me the grave danger of some of their teachings if taken to their logical conclusion. Their interpretation of Scripture was very limited and one-sided. He helped me to see what the Scriptures really say about the person and work of the Holy Spirit.

Finally, he made the most startling statement

15

about the Spirit that I had ever heard. He said, "Dave, whenever you hear someone who talks constantly about the Holy Spirit, you have reason to doubt that he really knows the Lord the way he should."

I could hardly believe my ears! How could anyone who talks about the Spirit be deficient or in error in his knowledge of God?

To back up his statement, the pastor turned to John 16:13-14 and read, "When the Spirit of truth comes : . . he will glorify me, for he will take what is mine and declare it unto you."

So that was it! The work of the Spirit is to glorify Christ, not himself. Thus the man who talks constantly about the Spirit, almost to the exclusion of Christ, may be showing that the Spirit has not really had a chance to do his work of glorifying Christ in the life of that person. The pastor elaborated further on the centrality of Christ in the Bible. The ministry of the Spirit will always bring Christ into the center.

I thought back on what my friends had said. They had talked at great length about the Spirit, but little about Christ. They had talked of their own experience, but little about the objective Word of God. This was what Bill had been trying to show me. Now God used this pastor to put it into focus for me. With a great sense of relief I returned home, went to bed and dropped off to a peaceful sleep.

Over the years, I have had abundant reason to be thankful for the teaching which my pastor gave me. The more I have thought about the main truth he taught me, the more meaningful it has become. In the following pages I will share some experiences in which a biblical understanding of the work of the Spirit was indispensable.

WHO IS THE HOLY SPIRIT?/ Even though the ministry of the Holy Spirit is to glorify Christ, God does want us to understand how the Spirit himself works so that we can respond intelligently to the Spirit's initiative. Consequently, from the first chapter of Genesis to the last chapter of Revelation, the Holy Spirit is very much present on the pages of Scripture. Our study is limited to considering his role in the world mission of the church. But in order to understand that role, it is necessary to take a brief look at who he is and what he does.

The Holy Spirit is a person. This is made clear, first of all, by his attributes. The Bible describes him as having intellect (Is. 11:2; 1 Cor. 2:10-11) and emotions. Thus he can be grieved (Is. 63:10; Eph. 4:30). He also has a will capable of making decisions according to his wishes.

Second, his personhood is made clear by his works. The Bible tells us that he teaches (Jn. 14:26; 16:13), leads (Rom. 8:14), comforts and counsels (Jn. 14:16, 26), intercedes (Rom. 8:26), convicts (Jn. 16:8), gives commands (Acts 8:29;

17

13:2) and forbids certain actions (Acts 16:7). All of these are activities of a person, not some impersonal force.

And finally, the Bible's use of personal pronouns underscores the fact that the Spirit is a person. The Bible refers to the Spirit as "he" (Jn. 15:26; 16:13-14), and the Spirit refers to himself with the first person pronoun (Acts 13:2).

Thus the Bible pictures the Holy Spirit as one who has intellect, emotion and will, who acts as a person and is referred to as a person.

The Holy Spirit is God. The deity of the Spirit is unmistakable throughout the Scriptures. He is identified with God in a variety of ways—through his titles, his attributes and his works. He is called the Spirit of God (Gen. 1:2),[1] the Spirit of the Lord of hosts (Zech. 7:12), the Spirit of the Lord (Lk. 4:18), the Spirit of Christ (Rom. 8:9), the Spirit of the living God (2 Cor. 3:3), the Spirit of God's Son (Gal. 4:6), the Spirit of glory and of God (1 Pet. 4:14).

When John baptized Jesus, the three Persons of the godhead were all present. God the Son was baptized, God the Father spoke from heaven with a voice and God the Spirit descended from heaven in visible form as a dove (Mt. 3:13-17). The relation of the three Persons is also seen in the baptismal formula used in the Great Commission, ". . . baptizing them in the name of the Father and of the Son and of the Holy Spirit" (Mt. 28:19).

The apostolic benediction also ties the three Persons together: "The grace of the Lord Jesus Christ and the love of God and the fellowship of the Holy Spirit be with you all" (2 Cor. 13:14).

Many of the attributes which can apply only to God are applied to the Holy Spirit in such a way as to indicate his oneness with the Father. He is eternal (Heb. 9:14). He is the Spirit of truth (Jn. 16:13), of life (Rom. 8:2), of love (Rom. 15:30), of holiness (Rom. 1:4). The very name "Holy Spirit," used so extensively in Scripture, underscores this latter attribute. He is omnipresent; the psalmist could find no way to flee from his presence (Ps. 139:7-12). He is omniscient and can comprehend the depths of God which no man can fathom (1 Cor. 2:10-11).

The Holy Spirit is spoken of interchangeably with God. For example, in Acts 5, Peter, after accusing Ananias and Sapphira of lying to the Holy Spirit (5:3), said a moment later that they had lied not to men but to God (5:4), implying that to lie to the Holy Spirit is to lie to God. Paul tells the Corinthians that they are God's temple in which his Spirit dwells (1 Cor. 3:16) and then says they are the temple of the Holy Spirit (1 Cor. 6:19).

WHAT IS THE WORK OF THE HOLY SPIRIT?/ The work of the Spirit, which is extensive and varied throughout Scripture, also indicates his deity. For the sake of clarity we will divide it into four areas for a brief overview.

The Spirit is active in the eternal purposes of God. He is active with God the Father in such activities as the creation, the giving of the written Word of God and the endowing of individuals for service.

In the creation story we read that "the Spirit of God was moving over the face of the waters" (Gen. 1:2). Job says, "By his wind [Spirit] the heavens were made fair" (Job 26:13), and "The Spirit of God has made me, and the breath of the Almighty gives me life" (Job 33:4). The psalmist adds, "When thou sendest forth thy Spirit, they are created" (Ps. 104:30).

The Bible itself is a product of the inspiration of the Spirit. This was recognized by the Old Testament prophets: "The Spirit of the Lord speaks by me, his word is upon my tongue" (2 Sam. 23:2; see also Is. 59:21). It was affirmed by Jesus Christ, who promised the Spirit would aid the men chosen to record what he had said. "But the Counselor, the Holy Spirit, whom the Father will send in my name, he will teach you all things, and bring to your remembrance all that I have said to you" (Jn. 14:26). It was recognized by the apostles Paul— "The Holy Spirit was right in saying to your fathers through Isaiah the prophet . . ." (Acts 28:25)—and Peter—"No prophecy ever came by the impulse of man, but men moved by the Holy Spirit spoke from God" (2 Pet. 1:21).

The Holy Spirit also illuminates the understanding of those who read the Scripture. "When
the Spirit of truth comes, he will guide you into all
the truth" (Jn. 16:13). "No one comprehends the
thoughts of God except the Spirit of God. Now we
have received not the spirit of the world, but the
Spirit which is from God, that we might understand the gifts bestowed on us by God" (1 Cor.
2:11-12). Thus the thoughts of God expressed in
Scripture, which are among his gifts bestowed on
us, are understandable only through the illumina-
tion of the Spirit of God.

Throughout history the Spirit has endowed
individuals for a special task placed upon them by
God. While this is not limited to biblical person-
alities, it is seen clearly in the following men. God
chose Bezalel to direct the building of the Taber-
nacle and said of him, "I have filled him with the
Spirit of God, with ability and intelligence, with
knowledge and all craftsmanship, to devise artistic
designs, to work in gold, silver and bronze, in cut-
ting stones for setting, and in carving wood, for
work in every craft" (Ex. 31:3-5). When God chose
Joshua to succeed Moses, God said to Moses,
"Take Joshua the son of Nun, a man in whom is
the spirit, and lay your hand upon him" (Num.
27:18).

When Gideon was raised up by God to deliver
Israel from the Midianites, "the Spirit of the Lord
took possession of Gideon" (Judg. 6:34). The most

renowned of all the judges in terms of physical feats was Samson. When he was just a boy, "the Spirit of the Lord began to stir him" (Judg. 13:25), and three times in his remarkable career "the Spirit of the Lord came mightily upon him" (Judg. 14:6, 19; 15:14). In each case it was to perform acts to deliver the people of God.

The Spirit played a significant role in the earthly life of Christ. Jesus was conceived in the womb of the virgin by the Holy Spirit (Mt. 1:20; Lk 1:35). The Spirit came upon him in bodily form at the time of his baptism (Mt. 3:16; Lk. 3:22) and led him into the wilderness to be tempted by the devil (Mt. 4:1).

Following his temptation Jesus returned "in the power of the Spirit into Galilee" (Lk. 4:14) to begin his public ministry. From the outset Jesus recognized that his power came from the Spirit, for in the synagogue in Nazareth he read from Isaiah, "The Spirit of the Lord is upon me, because he has anointed me to preach good news to the poor . . ." (Lk. 4:18). His miracles were performed through the Spirit: "If it is by the Spirit of God that I cast out demons, then the kingdom of God has come upon you" (Mt. 12:28).

The writer of Hebrews tells us that in his death Christ "through the eternal Spirit offered himself without blemish to God" (Heb. 9:14). In other words, the death of Christ was an act carried out through the power of the Spirit. So likewise was his resurrection. It was the Spirit who raised him from the dead. Paul refers in Romans 8:11 to "the Spirit of him who raised Jesus from the dead." And it was in the resurrection, accomplished through the Spirit, that Christ was proclaimed irrefutably as the Son of God. Paul says he was "designated Son of God in power according to the Spirit of holiness by his resurrection from the dead" (Rom. 1:4).

Thus, having been active in the birth of Christ, in his baptism, in his temptation, throughout his ministry, in his death and in his resurrection, it is not surprising that the present ministry of the Spirit is to glorify Christ, as we have already seen in John 16:14.

The Spirit has a specific ministry to those who do not follow Christ. He exercises a restraining influence in the world, although this may be withdrawn, as it was at the time of the Flood. "My spirit shall not abide in man forever, for he is flesh" (Gen. 6:3). In his restraining work he also convicts the unbeliever of sin. "When he comes, he will convince the world of sin and of righteousness and of judgment; of sin, because they do not believe in me; of righteousness, because I go to the Father, and you will see me no more; of judgment, because the ruler of this world is judged" (Jn. 16:8-11).

The Spirit is active in the life of a believer. At the moment of salvation, several things occur simultaneously. Based on his repentance and faith, the believer is regenerated by the Spirit. Christ said to Nicodemus, "Unless one is born anew, he cannot see the kingdom of God . . . unless one is born of water and the Spirit, he cannot enter the kingdom of God" (Jn. 3:3, 5). Paul says, "He has saved us, not because of deeds done by us in righteousness, but in virtue of his own mercy, by the washing of regeneration and renewal in the Holy Spirit, which he poured upon us richly through Jesus Christ our Savior" (Tit. 3:5-6).

Simultaneous with regeneration is the baptism of the Spirit. This is the act whereby a believer is baptized into the body of Christ and becomes a member of God's family. "For by one Spirit we were all baptized into one body—Jews or Greeks, slaves or free—and all were made to drink of one Spirit" (1 Cor. 12:13). (Chapter 2 treats this topic in more detail.)

Likewise the Spirit seals all who come to Christ. "In him you also who have heard the word of truth, the gospel of your salvation, and have believed in him, were sealed with the promised Holy Spirit, which is the guarantee of our inheritance until we acquire possession of it, to the praise of his glory" (Eph. 1:13-14). (See also 2 Cor. 1:22; Eph. 4:30.)

At the same time the Spirit takes up his dwelling place in the life of the believer. "But you are not in the flesh, you are in the Spirit, if the Spirit of God

really dwells in you. Any one who does not have
the Spirit of Christ does not belong to him. . . . If
the Spirit of him who raised Jesus from the dead
dwells in you, he who raised Christ Jesus from the
dead will give life to your mortal bodies also
through his Spirit which dwells in you" (Rom. 8:9,
11). (See also 1 Cor. 6:19; Gal. 4:6; 1 Jn. 4:13).

After he receives the Spirit at the moment of
salvation, the Christian must be filled repeatedly
with the Spirit. The Spirit gives gifts to believers
for their individual growth and for the edification
of the church, and manifests his fruit in the lives of
believers. This fruit is described by Paul as "love,
joy, peace, patience, kindness, goodness, faithfulness, gentleness, self control" (Gal. 5:22-23).

Finally, the Spirit intercedes for believers and
helps them in their prayer life. "Likewise the Spirit
helps us in our weakness; for we do not know how
to pray as we ought, but the Spirit himself intercedes for us with sighs too deep for words" (Rom.
8:26). (See also Eph. 2:18; 6:18; 1 Cor. 14:15;
Jude 20-21.)

With this brief survey of who the Holy Spirit is
and what he does, we turn now in more detail to
his specific ministries in the life of the believer and
in the life of the church for its world mission.

2
"BAPTIZED INTO ONE BODY"

Brother, would you be willing to pray with a group of us?

Of course I would. This was a group of earnest students at a college I was visiting. Some of them had recently experienced special gifts of the Spirit, and their eagerness to share these gifts with others was obvious. I suspected that the purpose of the prayer meeting might well be to impart one or another of these gifts to me. I was certainly willing to receive anything God wanted to give me so was glad to join them in prayer.

The girl who had spoken ushered me into a secluded classroom where several fellows had gathered for prayer. After I was introduced to each one she said, "Now let's all just praise God together."

The next ten or fifteen minutes were spent in worship and praise as we lifted our voices together to God. Some of the praise took the form of singing. At other times it was just a welling up of thanksgiving to God. Occasionally one of the students prayed quietly in tongues. Then the girl, who seemed to be the spokesman of the group, turned to me and said, "Are you ready now, brother, to receive the baptism of the Spirit?"

I replied, "I have received the baptism of the Spirit."

"When?"

"When I became a Christian."

"Oh, but that isn't what we mean."

I knew it wasn't what she had meant. She was using the phrase to refer to a subsequent experience she believed would take place in the life of the believer some time after his salvation. The evidence of this baptism, according to my friends, would be the sign of speaking in tongues. Unless I had demonstrated this sign, I had no evidence of having been baptized with the Spirit.

For the next two hours these students and I shared together our understanding of what the baptism of the Spirit is. Our time of prayer came to an end, because I was not willing to pray for something which I believed the Scriptures told me I already had received. To do so would have been to doubt that God had done for me what he said he would do when I received Christ. They, on the other hand, felt that my experience of the Spirit of God was deficient, because I had not had the outward evidence of speaking in tongues.

I recall another prayer meeting where the spontaneity of the believers was equally refreshing, and where their desires for me were equally sincere. The setting, however, was totally different. Instead of a classroom in a U.S. college, we were in the jungles of Colombia. Our "prayer room" was a sheltered glade in the lush tropical forests. The sounds of parrots and other multicolored birds provided background music. Several dozen Christians had gathered for an unhurried day of prayer and fasting, a weekly practice of theirs. Time was spent in study of the Word of God, interspersed with periods of prayer or singing and worship.

At one point in the afternoon several of them laid hands on me in earnest and fervent prayer, as they asked God to pour out his Spirit on me in all of his fullness. They prayed for my personal relationship to God, for my family and for my public ministry. Prayer and praise in tongues were used frequently that day, too, but no questions were asked nor petitions made for me to experience the same thing. They only asked that God would give me all he wished me to have. No one asked if I had been baptized with the Spirit. No one asked if I was ready to receive a new gift. This was left entirely to the sovereign act of the Spirit, whom they trusted to impart his gifts as he chose.

This scene was repeated many times during a period of years in Colombia, where it was my privilege to work closely with humble new believers, most of whom were unlettered peasants. Many of them received gifts from God that I never had. They never tried to force these on me. Rather, in love and brotherly fellowship they prayed for all of God's fullness in my life and ministry, and they used their gifts to edify me in the Lord. Frequently God spoke to my heart through them, even while they thought that I was ministering to them. My life was touched indelibly by these people, who knew more of the power and fruit of the Spirit of God than any group I had ever known.

As I compared these experiences involving equally sincere Christians, I began to see the importance of understanding the baptism of the Spirit. At times it might seem like nothing more than a problem of semantics. One person uses the phrase to refer to one experience; another uses it to refer to another experience. Why not accept each with his own definition? Or perhaps we all really mean the same thing but are expressing it in different ways.

In any matter related to doctrine, logic and experience may play a part in our understanding. But in the final analysis there is only one way to get to the root of it—the method Paul employed in dealing with doctrinal issues when he asked, " *But what does the scripture say?*" (Gal. 4:30). Unless we start with the Scripture, we run the grave risk of arguing solely on the basis of experience or logic, neither of which is adequate. The objective Word of God is our only final court of appeal. Therefore, we must study how the Bible uses the phrase "the baptism of the Spirit" if we are to understand its meaning.

In the New Testament seven passages mention the baptism of the Spirit, and we must examine each of these carefully. The seven cases may be divided into three categories: prophetic, historical and didactic.

PROPHETIC/ Five of the references are prophetic in nature. Four of them are in the statement made by John the Baptist which is recorded in each of the four gospels: "I baptize you with water for repentence, but he who is coming after me is mightier than I, whose sandals I am not worthy to carry; he will baptize you with the Holy Spirit and with fire" (Mt. 3:11). (See also Mk. 1:7-8; Lk. 3:16; Jn. 1:33.) This was a clear prophecy by John that Jesus Christ would baptize his followers with the Holy Spirit. John did not say when this would happen, simply that it *would* take place.

Jesus repeated John's statement immediately prior to his ascension, explaining that what was to happen in a few days would be the fulfillment of what John had prophesied: "And while he was staying with them he charged them not to depart from Jerusalem, but to wait for the promise of the Father, which, he said, 'You heard from me, for John baptized with water, but before many days you shall be baptized with the Holy Spirit' " (Acts 1:4-5). When on the day of Pentecost the disciples received the Holy Spirit, with the accompanying rush of wind and tongues of fire, it was understood that this prophecy was now fulfilled.

HISTORICAL/ One of the passages is historical in nature; that is, it refers back, in narrative form, to what had been prophesied by John and by Christ and then fulfilled on the day of Pentecost. When Peter preached the gospel to the household of a Gentile, Cornelius and his family received the Holy Spirit (Acts 10:44-48). When Peter returned to Jerusalem from Caesarea, he was called by the other apostles to explain what had happened. He told the story and then said:

As I began to speak, the Holy Spirit fell on them just as on us at the beginning. And I remembered the word of the Lord, how he said, "John baptized with water, but you shall be baptized with the Holy Spirit." If then God gave the same gift to them as he gave to us when we believed in the Lord Jesus Christ, who was I that I could withstand God? (Acts 11:15-17)

Peter thus explained that the initial reception of the Holy Spirit by Cornelius and his family was the same thing that had happened on the day of Pentecost, "when we believed in the Lord Jesus Christ." At the moment of belief the Holy Spirit was given. Peter took this to be the fulfillment of the prophecies of John and Jesus announcing that they would be baptized with the Holy Spirit. The baptism with the Holy Spirit took place simultaneously with their belief.

Of the seven passages where the baptism of the Holy Spirit is mentioned, the first six all refer to the same event, namely, the experience of Pentecost. That was the moment when the Holy Spirit came to take up his dwelling in the believers. This was the birth of the true church of Jesus Christ. It was the moment when the followers of Christ were baptized with the Holy Spirit. But what does this baptism mean?

DIDACTIC/ It remains for the one final passage in the New Testament which refers to this baptism to give us a doctrinal explanation of its meaning. In 1 Corinthians 12:13, Paul writes, "For by one Spirit we were all baptized into one body—Jews or Greeks, slaves or free—and all were made to drink of one Spirit." We must take this verse, like any verse in the Bible, in its context if we are to understand its meaning. Several factors become plain when we study the entire context of 1 Corinthians 12.

First, *the unity of all Christians* is the major

33

thrust of what Paul is saying in this passage. Notice the emphasis in these phrases: "the same Spirit" (vv. 4, 8, 9); "one Spirit" (vv. 9, 13—twice in this latter verse); "one and the same Spirit" (v. 11); "the same Lord" (v. 5); "the same God" (v. 6); "the common good" (v. 7); "the body is one" (v. 12); "one body" (v. 12, 13); "there are many parts, yet one body" (v. 20); "that there may be no discord in the body" (v. 25).

The entire picture Paul paints of the body speaks of unity. He shows how a physical body, while made up of many members, is yet one unit that must function as a whole. "So it is with Christ" (v. 12). Even though the different parts of the body have their individual functions, they must work together for the good of the entire body. They cannot expel anyone from the body. "The eye cannot say to the hand, 'I have no need of you,' nor again the head to the feet, 'I have no need of you' " (v. 21). Nor can any member withdraw from the body. "If the foot should say, 'Because I am not a hand, I do not belong to the body,' that would not make it any less a part of the body. And if the ear should say, 'Because I am not an eye, I do not belong to the body,' that would not make it any less a part of the body" (vv. 15-16).

In this context of unity Paul says, "For by one Spirit we were all baptized into one body—Jews or Greeks, slaves or free—and all were made to drink of one Spirit." John R. W. Stott points out in this connection, "So the baptism of the Spirit in this verse, far from being a dividing factor (some have it, others have not), is the great uniting factor (an experience we have all had)."[1] There are not two bodies of Christ, those who have been baptized with the Spirit and those who yet await the baptism. Paul knows no such dichotomy.

Second, and closely related to the above, Paul emphasizes *the universality of this experience for all believers.* The use of the word *all* is decisive. "We were *all* baptized into one body . . . and *all* were made to drink of one Spirit." This is not an experience which some have had and others must seek, nor is it something which comes subsequent to salvation and is dependent on certain conditions. It is something which has happened to *all* who bear the name of Christ, whether they be Jews or Greeks, slaves or free, Corinthians or New Yorkers. This verse cannot be stretched to imply that Paul is referring to the baptism with the Spirit as something which not all Christians have yet experienced. Quite the opposite. His references to *all* are conclusive. This is a universal experience which every Christian has passed through. Anyone who has not been baptized with the Spirit is not yet a Christian.

It should be noted here that the Greek preposition *en,* translated in the Revised Standard Version as "by," is the same word used in the other six references to the baptism of the Spirit. In all the other passages it is translated "with." Thus, it would be more consistent to translate 1 Corinthians 12:13, "For *with* one Spirit we were all baptized. . . ." This is important in relation to the next point.

Third, *the symbol of baptism illustrates what takes place in salvation.* Stott points out that in every kind of baptism there are four parts: the subject, who does the baptizing; the object, who receives the baptism; the element, with which baptism is administered; and the purpose, for which baptism is administered. For example, in the Christian rite of baptism the minister (subject) baptizes the believer (object) in water (element) into the name of the Father, the Son and the Holy Spirit (purpose).

By the same token, spiritual baptism is explained in 1 Corinthians 12. Christ (the subject) baptizes the believer (object) with the Spirit (element) into the body of Christ (purpose). This fulfills precisely what was prophesied, "He will baptize you with the Holy Spirit" (Mt. 3:11 et al.).

Therefore, *the purpose of the baptism with the Holy Spirit is to incorporate the believer into the body of Christ.* This is not something which waits for a period of time following salvation. Rather it is simultaneous with salvation. As soon as a person commits himself to Jesus Christ, in repentance and faith, he becomes a Christian and automatically a member of the body of Christ. He receives the

Holy Spirit into his life. He cannot be a Christian
without having the Holy Spirit, who has been the
means of his incorporation into the church. "Any
one who does not have the Spirit of Christ does
not belong to him" (Rom. 8:9). If we belong to
Christ, we have the Spirit and do not need to seek
a further baptism. This has already taken place at
the moment of conversion.

The use of the aorist tense in the two verbs of 1
Corinthians 12:13 ("baptized" and "made to
drink") indicates a past action which took place
once and for all and need not be repeated. This
places the baptism with the Spirit in its proper
place historically in the life of the believer.

Thus Paul's emphasis on the unity of the body,
the universality of the baptism experience for all
believers and the very symbolism of baptism makes
clear what he is talking about. He is referring to
that which takes place at the moment of salvation
when Jesus Christ, receiving the repentant sinner
who has expressed faith in him, regenerates that
sinner and baptizes him with the Spirit to make
him part of his body, the church.

In conclusion one more point is worthy of note.
*We look in vain in the New Testament for any
command to be baptized with the Holy Spirit.* If
the baptism with the Spirit were a vital and integral
step in Christian growth (as some would have us
believe), it is inconceivable that no New Testament
writer, nor Christ himself, would ever exhort us to

be baptized or to seek such a baptism with the Spirit. The reason is simple: We are not commanded, as Christians, to seek something which has already taken place in our lives. Thus when my friends asked if I were ready to receive the baptism of the Spirit, my reply was that I had already received it at the moment of salvation. This was not a presumptuous boast. It was a recognition and acceptance of what Christ had done for me through his Spirit when I received him.

In contrast to the fact that there is no command to be baptized with the Spirit, there *is* a clear command to "be filled with the Spirit" (Eph. 5:18). This important contrast leads us immediately to a discussion of the fullness of the Spirit.

3

"BE FILLED
WITH THE
SPIRIT"

The Ephesian Christians were a growing and mature group of believers. The theme which Paul takes up in his letter to them indicates that they were more ready for strong meat than some other churches. When he wrote to the Corinthians, for example, he was not able to write to them as "spiritual men" but rather as "men of the flesh"; he had to feed them with "milk" rather than with "solid food" (1 Cor. 3:1-3). Not so the Ephesians. With them he was able to discuss deeper issues. He did not have to berate them for their carnal practices.

Yet it was to the Ephesians that he gave the command, "And do not get drunk with wine . . . but be filled with the Spirit" (Eph. 5:18). Why should he have to tell mature Christians to be filled with the Spirit? One reason is that while the believer has been set free through the blood of Christ from the penalty of sin, he still lives within the limitations of the flesh and is capable of sinning. John, in writing to Christians, recognized this when he said, "If we say we have no sin, we deceive ourselves, and the truth is not in us" (1 Jn. 1:8). When a believer does sin, the Holy Spirit does not leave him, but he certainly is not a Spirit-filled Christian at that moment. While still possessing the Spirit, he needs a fresh infilling of the Spirit. Even mature Christians will not always be Spirit-filled Christians. Therefore, Paul exhorts the Ephesians to "be filled with the Spirit."

A second reason Christians need repeated fillings is to be empowered for witness. The book of Acts gives some striking illustrations of the fullness of the Spirit in the lives of Christians as they witnessed to non-Christians. We must never fall into the trap of assuming that everything that happened in Acts is normative for the Christian life and is to be sought or expected in the life of all believers. Acts is a historical narrative that describes what happened to specific individuals at a given point in the history of the church. Some of these experiences may be repeated throughout church history. Others may not. Nevertheless Acts does give a picture of how the Spirit of God has worked. With this in mind it will help our understanding of this topic to look at the passages in Acts where men were filled with the Spirit.

This will be particularly relevant to our purpose in this book, which is to study the work of the Holy Spirit as it relates to the world mission of the church. Acts portrays for us the beginnings of that outreach. Therefore, an understanding of how the Spirit worked during that period will clarify some of his methods.

THE DAY OF PENTECOST/

When the day of Pentecost had come, they were all together in one place. And suddenly a sound came from heaven like the rush of a mighty wind, and it filled all the house where they were sitting. And there appeared to them tongues as of fire, distributed and resting on each one of them. And they were all filled with the Holy Spirit and began to speak in other tongues, as the Spirit gave them utterance. (Acts 2:1-4)

This was the initial giving of the Holy Spirit. It was, as we have seen, the fulfillment of the prophecy of John the Baptist and the promise of Christ. What happened in these verses is important to our understanding of the Holy Spirit's work.

The first result of the Spirit's coming into the lives of the Christians was that they all began to speak. The fact that they spoke in tongues is important and will be discussed in a later chapter. However, for our purposes here we want to focus on what they said, rather than on how they said it. The content of their speaking is, therefore, significant. Those who heard the Christians speaking said, "Are not all these who are speaking Galileans? And how is it that we hear, each of us in his own native language? ... we hear them telling in our own tongues the mighty works of God" (Acts 2:7-8, 11).

"The mighty works of God" was the theme of their message! The first result of being filled with the Spirit, then, was that they shared the good news of what God was doing. And as they shared, many believed. As a result of their testimony, supported by Peter's great sermon recorded in Acts 2:14-40, about three thousand people placed their trust in Christ as the Messiah. This sets a pattern for the rest of the book of Acts, as we shall see in the following passages.

PETER BEFORE THE COUNCIL/

On the morrow their rulers and elders and scribes were gathered together in Jerusalem, with Annas the high priest and Caiaphas and John and Alexander, and all who were of the high-priestly family. And when they had set them in the midst, they inquired, "By what power or by what name did you do this?" Then Peter, filled with the Holy Spirit, said to them, "Rulers of the people and elders, if we are being examined today concerning a good deed done to a cripple, by what means this man has been healed, be it known to you all and the people of Israel, that by the name of Jesus Christ of Nazareth, whom you crucified, whom God raised from the dead, by him this man is standing before you well. This is the stone which was rejected by you builders, but which has become the head of the corner. And there is salvation in no one else, for there is no other name under heaven given among men by which we must be saved. (Acts 4:5-12)

Here is Peter, who had been filled with the Spirit on the day of Pentecost, being filled again. Why? Because a fresh infilling was necessary to face a specific task that fell to him. He was in court for "proclaiming in Jesus the resurrection from the dead," which was annoying the Jews (4:1-3). The healing of the lame man at the gate of the temple had triggered his arrest, but the real issue was his preaching.

It is a great thing to see bold witness in the face of threats. I had a friend in Colombia named Lupercio Taba who was a fearless pastor. One Sunday he was preaching from his pulpit when a man appeared at a side window of the church, aimed a pistol at Lupercio and ordered him to stop preaching. The congregation, seeing the danger, dove to the floor and hid under the pews. Lupercio, however, never flinched. He went right on preaching the gospel. The man fired four shots at him. Two

43

shots went past his head, one on one side, one on the other, and lodged in the wall behind him. Two shots went past his body, one under one arm, one under the other, and also lodged in the wall. The would-be assassin then dropped his gun and fled. Lupercio, still unmoved, continued his sermon.

Such a reaction is not natural, to put it mildly. It could only have been a special filling of the Holy Spirit which enabled him to face the danger of death with unflinching coolness and continue the preaching of the Word with boldness.

THE CHOICE OF DEACONS/ In the course of time a complaint arose against the apostles, because the Hellenic widows were being neglected. The apostles recognized the problem and the justice of the complaint. But they did not feel they could leave their ministry in order to wait on tables. So they decided to choose special men for this task.

And the twelve summoned the body of disciples and said, "It is not right that we should give up preaching the word of God to serve tables. Therefore, brethren, pick out from among you seven men of good repute, full of the Spirit and of wisdom, whom we may appoint to this duty. But we will devote ourselves to prayer and to the ministry of the word." (Acts 6:2-4)

It is significant that one of the requirements for waiting on tables was that the men be "full of the

Spirit." Even a duty such as this required a Spirit-filled man.

> *And they chose Stephen, a man full of faith and of the Holy Spirit, and Philip, and Prochorus, and Nicanor, and Timon, and Parmenas, and Nicolaus. . . . And the word of God increased; and the number of the disciples multiplied greatly in Jerusalem, and a great many of the priests were obedient to the faith. (Acts 6:5, 7)*

Once again when men were filled with the Holy Spirit the direct result was the spreading of the Word of God.

THE MARTYRDOM OF STEPHEN/ Stephen, although chosen primarily for the menial task of waiting on tables, was a man "full of grace and power, [who] did great wonders and signs among the people" (Acts 6:8). This called forth violent opposition from the enemies of the gospel. Before long Stephen was arrested and falsely accused. Being filled with the Spirit he was enabled to present his defense in a powerful and convincing address in which he traced the Old Testament history which had prepared the way for the coming of the Messiah (Acts 7:1-53). When he came to the climax of his defense and accused the Jews of resisting the Holy Spirit and murdering the Righteous One, they turned on him to stone him to death.

> *But he, full of the Holy Spirit, gazed into heaven*

and saw the glory of God, and Jesus standing at the right hand of God. . . . And as they were stoning Stephen, he prayed, "Lord Jesus, receive my spirit." And he knelt down and cried with a loud voice, "Lord, do not hold this sin against them." And when he had said this, he fell asleep. (Acts 7:55, 59-60)

Although Stephen had already been identified as a man full of the Holy Spirit, God now gave him a special infilling to enable him to face the crisis of death. Stephen was able to pray for the forgiveness of his murderers—a response quite beyond normal human capacities yet one which demonstrated the heart of the gospel of love.

And the result? A young man named Saul was standing by holding the coats of the murderers. He no doubt heard these words. This incident must have been a link in the chain that ultimately brought this young man to Christ. We know him today as Paul the Apostle, the great missionary leader of the early church. So once again the fullness of the Spirit resulted in a direct witness and further outreach of the gospel.

THE CONVERSION OF SAUL/ When Saul of Tarsus was stopped by the Lord on the Damascus road, a dramatic scene developed—with a sudden light, a voice from heaven and ensuing blindness. Three days later, while Saul was still blind, God sent Ananias to minister to him. Ananias said,

*"Brother Saul, the Lord Jesus who appeared to
you on the road by which you came, has sent
me that you may regain your sight and be filled
with the Holy Spirit." And immediately something like scales fell from his eyes and he re-
gained his sight. Then he rose and was baptized,
and took food and was strengthened. For several
days he was with the disciples at Damascus. And
in the synagogues immediately he proclaimed
Jesus, saying, "He is the Son of God." (Acts
9:17-20)*

While the text does not actually say that Saul
was filled with the Holy Spirit, it clearly implies
that he was. Ananias said he was sent so that Saul
might be filled with the Spirit, and the fact that
Saul came to Christ at this point is reason enough
to believe he became Spirit-filled. As we have seen,
conversion and baptism with the Spirit are simultaneous. So we know that Saul was baptized with the
Spirit into the body of Christ. And what was the
result? "Immediately he proclaimed Jesus. . . ."
The same pattern held true. A man was filled with
the Spirit and began to speak about Jesus and
spread the message of the gospel.

BARNABAS AT ANTIOCH/ When the gospel
had spread as far as Antioch and the church had
begun to grow there, news of this reached the
apostles in Jerusalem. They decided to send Barnabas to Antioch to help the new Christians get

established in their faith. When Barnabas arrived, he rejoiced to see the grace of God at work. We read that Barnabas "was a good man, full of the Holy Spirit and of faith. And a large company was added to the Lord" (Acts 11:24).

Note that last phrase. It develops the same pattern we have seen in all the previous cases. When a man is filled with the Spirit, the Word goes out, and people are added to the Lord.

PAUL AND ELYMAS/ When Paul and Barnabas set out on their first missionary journey, they came to Cyprus, where they encountered their first opposition in the person of Elymas, a sorcerer who "withstood them, seeking to turn away the proconsul from the faith" (Acts 13:8). God knew that in order to combat the forces of evil that wanted to hinder the gospel, Paul would need a special filling of the Holy Spirit. So he gave it to him.

But Saul, who is also called Paul, filled with the Holy Spirit, looked intently at him and said, "You son of the devil, you enemy of all righteousness, full of all deceit and villainy, will you not stop making crooked the straight paths of the Lord? And now, behold, the hand of the Lord is upon you, and you shall be blind and unable to see the sun for a time." Immediately mist and darkness fell upon him and he went about seeking people to lead him by the hand. Then the proconsul believed, when he saw what had occurred, for he was astonished at the teaching of the Lord. (Acts 13:9-12)

This incident gives a slightly different perspective on the fullness of the Spirit and the witness of Christians. In this case Paul was filled with the Spirit in order to rebuke someone who opposed the spread of the gospel. His approach was direct and uncompromising. He minced no words. His language was hardly calculated to win friends and influence people. It is doubtful that most books on personal evangelism would recommend this approach! Nevertheless it is well to remember that he spoke these words under the power of the Spirit. There are times when such a rebuke is necessary. It was an integral part of witness. And, as in previous instances, the result was that the proconsul believed.

THE DISCIPLES AT ICONIUM

And the word of the Lord spread throughout all the region. But the Jews incited the devout women of high standing and the leading men of the city, and stirred up persecution against Paul and Barnabas, and drove them out of their district. But they shook off the dust from their feet against them, and went to Iconium. And the disciples were filled with joy and with the Holy Spirit. Now at Iconium they entered together into the Jewish synagogue, and so spoke that a great company believed, both of Jews and of

Greeks. . . . So they remained for a long time, speaking boldly for the Lord, who bore witness to the word of his grace. . . . (Acts 13:49—14:3) In the face of persecution the disciples continued their witness joyfully, because they were filled with the Holy Spirit. And, true to the pattern, a great company believed.

I knew a man in Colombia who was so aggressive in his witness, even in the face of fierce persecution, that local authorities finally threw him in prison. He joyfully continued to witness for Christ to the other prisoners, leading some of them to salvation. The authorities pondered this for a while, and finally decided it would be best to release him before he had the entire jail converted! This kind of witness can only be the result of the fullness of the Holy Spirit.

CONCLUSION/ In chapter 2 we concluded that the baptism of the Holy Spirit is a once-for-all transaction which takes place at the moment of salvation. It never needs to be repeated, and, therefore, we find no command to be baptized with the Spirit. The fullness of the Spirit, however, is something which must be repeated throughout the life of a Christian because the sinful nature of man will at times quench the Spirit in the life of the believer. The command in Ephesians 5:18 is in the present tense, meaning that it could legitimately be translated, "Keep on being filled with the Spirit."

In the cases in Acts we have studied in this chapter, those who were initially filled on the day of Pentecost were filled in a special way when a critical need arose. In every case in Acts where individuals or groups were filled with the Spirit the result was always the same: The Word of God went out in witness to unbelievers. Thus we can conclude that fullness of the Holy Spirit is the key to the outreach of the church with the message of Jesus Christ.

4

"YOU SHALL RECEIVE POWER"

We were sitting on a log in the forests of Colombia. To one side of us was a small clearing with a few scattered thatched-roof houses that composed the tiny village of Corozalito with a population of less than one hundred people. To the other side a great wall of jungle rose up before us with its massive trees, tangled vines and lush tropical foliage. Brilliantly colored parrots punctuated the air with their periodic screeches. An occasional monkey might be seen or heard as he swung through the vines.

My companion, Victor Landero, turned to me as we discussed the Scriptures together and said, "Brother, I've been concerned recently about the commands of Christ to evangelize. To the best of our ability we have been obeying the command in Mark 16:15, 'Go into all the world and preach the gospel to the whole creation.' But what bothered me was the following promise, 'And these signs will accompany those who believe: in my name they will cast out demons; they will speak in new tongues; they will pick up serpents, and if they drink any deadly thing, it will not hurt them; they will lay their hands on the sick, and they will recover.' I began to ask God why we were not seeing these signs accompanying our witness. And God has begun to show them to us."

The village of Corozalito itself was a testimony to the truth of Victor's claim that they had been attempting to obey Mark 16:15. At that time there were ninety-four people living there. Ninety-two of them were now Christians—every one as a result of Victor's faithful witness. He was a humble farmer with no education or training. He was also a new Christian who could not contain the joy of his newfound faith. It overflowed in a spontaneous witness to all with whom he had contact. Although he had never been to school, he had somehow taught himself to read. And now he was saturating himself with the Word of God, as he read it avidly, although slowly and haltingly.

Victor went on to explain that up to that moment he and other Christians there had already seen three of these signs fulfilled in their ministry (casting out demons, speaking in new tongues and laying hands on the sick for healing).

"One of these days one of our people will be bitten by a snake, and he won't die. [Poisonous snake bites are commonplace in that area of Colombia, and fatalities are all too frequent.] God will protect him. Then, one of our children will drink something poisonous by mistake, and he won't die either. We are fully expecting to see all five signs fulfilled soon through the Holy Spirit as a result of our obedience in preaching the gospel to the whole creation."

It would have been possible to enter into a discussion of the textual problems of including Mark 16:9-20 as part of the original text of Mark's gospel. I am well aware of the critical problems here and that its inclusion in the text is disputed by competent scholars. However, to try to explain to a new Christian, who could barely read, the intricacies of textual criticism, the problems of certain texts being included or excluded from the most reliable manuscripts, and all the implications arising from this seemed quite beyond the pale of our considerations. Victor had in front of him the widely accepted, standard Spanish text (roughly equivalent to the Revised Standard Version in English), which includes Mark 16:9-20 without so much as a footnote to raise the textual question. He was accepting at face value what he saw as the Word of God and was trying to act accordingly.

While Victor was as yet a new Christian who had

not had much opportunity for teaching from others, he was already seeing a vital connection between the work of the Holy Spirit and the commands of Jesus Christ for world evangelism. This connection is a significant truth that needs to be understood. As we saw in the last chapter, whenever the Holy Spirit filled Christians in the early church, the result was an outreach in gospel witness. One might wonder if the work of the Holy Spirit in world evangelism began with Pentecost. It is important to notice that the Holy Spirit, being one with the Father and the Son, was active *before* Pentecost in laying the foundation for worldwide witness.

Luke makes an interesting observation in his prologue to Acts: "In the first book, O Theophilus, I have dealt with all that Jesus began to do and teach, until the day when he was taken up, *after he had given commandment through the Holy Spirit to the apostles whom he had chosen*" (Acts 1:1-2). Thus, the Holy Spirit is directly linked to Christ's giving commands to the apostles. The context here seems to imply that this commandment was specifically the Great Commission that he gave several times during the period between the resurrection and the ascension. Even if his instructions were not limited to this command, they certainly included it.

Dr. Harry Boer has highlighted the relationship of the Holy Spirit to the Great Commission and

the outreach of the church in his classic work,
Pentecost and Missions. He says,

> The Great Commission played a powerful role in
> the missionary witness of the early church from
> the day of Pentecost to the present. It can be
> said that it always has been, is now, and always
> will be the heart and soul of all true missionary
> witness. But its meaning for and place in the life
> of the missionary community must, we believe,
> be differently construed than is customarily
> done. The Great Commission . . . derives its
> meaning and power wholly and exclusively from
> the Pentecost event.[1]

Boer develops skillfully the idea that the early
church received its primary motivation for mission
outreach through the coming of the Holy Spirit
rather than through the Great Commission. At the
same time, however, it is important to see that the
work of the Holy Spirit in the outreach of the
early church is based on the commands given by
Christ for world evangelism. Boer recognizes this
when he says that it was Pentecost that gave
meaning and power to the Great Commission.

So we turn now to the passages where the Great
Commission was given so that we can note the
relationship of the Holy Spirit to these commands.
We shall consider them in chronological order.

THE EVENING OF THE RESURRECTION DAY/
Then he said to them, "These are my words

57

which I spoke to you, while I was still with you, that everything written about me in the law of Moses and the prophets and the psalms must be fulfilled." Then he opened their minds to understand the scriptures, and said to them, "Thus it is written, that the Christ should suffer and on the third day rise from the dead, and that repentance and forgiveness of sins should be preached in his name to all nations, beginning from Jerusalem. You are witnesses of these things. And behold, I send the promise of my Father upon you; but stay in the city, until you are clothed with power from on high." (Lk. 24:44-49)

On the evening of the resurrection day, Christ met with his disciples as a group for the first time since before the crucifixion. While he had seen a few individuals during that day, this was his first meeting with the whole group. It is significant that the first thing he chose to speak about was the responsibility that was now to be theirs in preaching repentance and forgiveness of sins among all nations. As he gave them this charge, he also gave them a promise. He told them to do something for which they were not yet equipped, but he promised to provide the power necessary to carry out this task.

This, of course, was the promise of the Holy Spirit. The disciples were to remain in Jerusalem until this was fulfilled. But once it was fulfilled, they were to move out in obedience to the command, preaching in his name among all nations. Thus from the first the promise of the Holy Spirit was an integral part of the commission.

In John 20, John describes the same setting which Luke portrays:

On the evening of that day, the first day of the week, the doors being shut where the disciples were, for fear of the Jews, Jesus came and stood among them and said to them, "Peace be with you." When he had said this, he showed them his hands and his side. Then the disciples were glad when they saw the Lord. Jesus said to them again, "Peace be with you. As the Father has sent me, even so I send you." And when he had said this, he breathed on them, and said to them, "Receive the Holy Spirit." (Jn. 20:19-22)

The disciples were gathered together on the evening of the resurrection day, when Jesus appeared and spoke to them. The words that John records Jesus as saying are quite distinct from those Luke mentions, yet the substance is the same in both Gospels. While it is possible that Luke and John are simply recording the same command but using different words, the wide difference in the words makes this improbable. It is more likely that Jesus said in substance the same thing twice the same evening so that the disciples would not miss the point.

There has been much debate among theologians

and commentators about what happened when Jesus breathed on them. Did the disciples receive the Holy Spirit at that moment? Or was this a promise that they would receive him at the proper time? It seems to me that the answer lies in Jesus' promise to them forty days later that "before many days you shall be baptized with the Holy Spirit" (Acts 1:5). In other words, they had not yet received him. What he said in John was a promise of that which was still to come and which was fulfilled at Pentecost.

Regardless of whether or not one agrees with this interpretation, one fact is undebatable. When Jesus gave his commission as recorded in John, he tied it in immediately with the power which he would give them through the Holy Spirit to enable them to carry out this task. Thus the promise of the Holy Spirit was present in the commission.

ON A MOUNTAIN IN GALILEE/

Now the eleven disciples went to Galilee, to the mountain to which Jesus had directed them. And when they saw him they worshiped him; but some doubted. And Jesus came and said to them, "All authority in heaven and on earth has been given to me. Go therefore and make disciples of all nations, baptizing them in the name of the Father and of the Son and of the Holy Spirit, teaching them to observe all that I have commanded you; and lo, I am with you always,

to the close of the age." (Mt. 28:16-20)
This incident took place sometime after the
resurrection day. This is obvious from the fact that
it occurs in Galilee on a mountain, rather than in
Jerusalem in a room. Jesus appeared again to his
disciples and repeated his commission to them.
Although he does not specifically repeat the
promise of the Holy Spirit, he does refer to the
Spirit as being part of the whole picture. His command to baptize "in the name of the Father and of
the Son and of the Holy Spirit" shows that the
three persons of the godhead were related to the
command for world evangelism.

A PROMISE OF "SIGNS"/
*Afterward he appeared to the eleven themselves
as they sat at table; and he upbraided them for
their unbelief and hardness of heart, because
they had not believed those who saw him after
he had risen. And he said to them, "Go into all
the world and preach the gospel to the whole
creation. He who believes and is baptized will be
saved; but he who does not believe will be con-
demned. And these signs will accompany those
who believe: in my name they will cast out
demons; they will speak in new tongues; . . .
(Mk. 16:14-17)*
The time and place of this incident is not clear,
but since it involves a post-resurrection statement
of the Great Commission, we consider it here.

As mentioned above, a problem of textual criticism comes in here. If one accepts the widely held belief that the most reliable manuscripts do not include Mark 16:9-20, the discussion ends there. However, since many Christians base some of their views about the spiritual gifts on these verses, it is appropriate to comment here on the implications of the passage. (See also chapter 9 for a fuller discussion.)

Even if Jesus did speak of "signs" which would accompany the preaching and receiving of the truth, to suggest he meant that each of these signs would follow every time the gospel is preached is absurd. For example, how could this be fulfilled in areas of the world where there are no snakes? Or, every time the gospel is preached must someone drink deadly poison in order to fulfill this? Rather, what Christ said was that signs would be in evidence. The fact that my friend Victor wanted to see all of these signs in his own ministry was due to his refreshing way of accepting the Word of God at face value. In simple faith he expected God to do what God said he would do.

These signs correspond with some of the gifts of the Spirit described elsewhere in the New Testament. (See Rom. 12, 1 Cor. 12 and Eph. 4. See also the discussion in chapter 7.) Therefore, it is safe to assume that Christ was promising that the Holy Spirit would confirm their preaching by supernatural means. And this is precisely what happened, according to both Mark 16:20 and the book of Acts.

So once again the Holy Spirit was portrayed as active in the Great Commission and its implications for the church.

JESUS' LAST WORDS/

So when they had come together, they asked him, "Lord, will you at this time restore the kingdom to Israel?" He said to them, "It is not for you to know times or seasons which the Father has fixed by his own authority. But you shall receive power when the Holy Spirit has come upon you; and you shall be my witnesses in Jerusalem and in all Judea and Samaria and to the end of the earth." And when he had said this, as they were looking on, he was lifted up, and a cloud took him out of their sight. And while they were gazing into heaven as he went, behold, two men stood by them in white robes, and said, "Men of Galilee, why do you stand looking into heaven? This Jesus, who was taken up from you into heaven, will come in the same way as you saw him go into heaven." (Acts 1:6-11)

Here we find the last thing that Christ ever said to his disciples, as evidenced by the fact that as soon as he had said it, he was taken up to heaven. It is significant that he chose as his final words the commission to be witnesses to the end of the earth.

This places profound importance on that command. He must have known that his last words would be remembered more clearly than anything else he said to them. So he chose this all-important issue as the substance of this final statement.

And once again the promise of the Holy Spirit was an integral part of the commission.

In summary, Christ gave his Great Commission at least three times, if not more. He gave it on the day of the resurrection, probably repeating it twice that night in different words (Lk. 24 and Jn. 20). He gave it again in Galilee on a mountain (Mt. 28). When and where he gave it in Mark is not stated; this could conceivably have been a different time, or it could have been any one of the incidents in the other Gospels. Finally, he gave it as the final words immediately prior to his ascension.

It is well to remember, as Luke tells us in Acts 1:2, that "he had given commandment *through the Holy Spirit* to the apostles." That is, the power of the Holy Spirit and the giving of the command by Christ are directly related. And the command includes the promise of the Holy Spirit as the power to carry out the task. The task is a big one—as wide as the world itself in its scope. But the power to carry it out is the power of the one who created the world in the first place.

5
"SENT OUT
BY THE
HOLY SPIRIT"

The dream did not seem particularly out of the ordinary. Victor Landero had seen a certain house in the dream. It had a small fence in front with a gate and two gateposts, a thatched roof and other features common to many houses in that area of the forest. Victor, however, had never seen this particular house before. The one distinguishing element of the dream was that Victor heard a voice saying, "The people in that house are dying without Christ, because no one ever told them of him." This was repeated twice in the short dream. Then Victor woke up.

"Just another dream," he thought to himself as he tried to put it from his mind. But day after day, for weeks that stretched into months, he kept hearing that voice speaking of those people who were dying without Christ. Could it be that God was trying to say something to him?

Finally, after eight months of trying to forget the dream, Victor told the Lord that if the Lord really wanted him to find that house and tell those people of Christ, he would go. He had not the remotest idea where the house might be. But he took a companion and started off through the woods to look for it. They spent the first night in the home of a friend and continued their journey the next morning.

About noontime of the second day they came out into a clearing in the woods. There stood the house exactly as Victor had seen it in his dream, down to the last detail! When he recounted this story to me, I showed surprise at this point. But he said, "I wasn't surprised. I knew that house had to be there somewhere, and that God would guide me to it."

After knocking on the door, he explained to the lady of the house that he would like permission to invite her neighbors into her house that night and talk to them. A rather odd request coming from a total stranger! Surprisingly, however, she gave permission. She was so astounded at the request that she could scarcely speak. And she had good reason to be surprised. Three days before his arrival she, too, had had a strange dream. She saw her little home jammed with people from wall to wall. A man she had never seen was standing before them with an open book in his hand talking about something he called "the gospel" (which she had never heard of before). He also taught them some "gospel songs." Three days later Victor arrived and her dream came true!

Victor invited the neighbors from the surrounding countryside, and twenty-four of them showed up to fill the one-room house. After his explanation of the message of salvation, Victor asked how many would like to receive Christ. Every hand went up. He was sure they had misunderstood him, so he started over and gave the whole message again. Then a second time he asked how many would like to receive Christ. Again every hand went up.

"Yes! This is exactly what we want! We have never heard this before, but it is what we have been looking for."

So after prayer Victor invited them back the next night and suggested they bring their friends. Thirty-four showed up that night, all the original twenty-four plus ten new ones. All ten of the newcomers received Christ that night. Thirty-four new believers in two nights!

Victor stayed on for a few days and gave them some basic instruction in the Scriptures. Leaving a Bible with them, he returned home.

Less than a year later I visited that village, called Nueva Esperanza, an appropriate name since it means "New Hope." By the time of my visit there were about fifty believers. All thirty-four of the original ones were still faithfully following the Lord, and they had won other friends to Christ. Although most of them were illiterate, they would gather every night for Bible study and prayer under a little thatched roof held up by four posts which served as their chapel. Those who could read would read the Bible to the group. Then they would discuss it together, sing some hymns and join in united prayer. Here was a church in the New Testament sense of the word: "For where two or three are gathered in my name, there am I in the midst of them" (Mt. 18:20).

When I saw what had happened in Nueva Esperanza, and when I joined in family worship in the home Victor had seen in his dream, I could only rejoice in the leading of the Holy Spirit. This was a classic case of the Spirit leading an obedient believer into an outreach with the gospel. The fact that God used a dream to accomplish this should not be surprising. If he gave Peter a vision prior to leading him to Cornelius, and if he gave Cornelius a vision to tell him to send for Peter (see Acts 10), thus bringing about a new outreach with the gospel, why can he not do that today in Colombia if he so chooses?

A study of Acts reveals the remarkable ways in which the Holy Spirit worked in the early church to spread the gospel. There are well over fifty references to the Spirit in Acts, causing some to call this book "The Acts of the Holy Spirit." We shall now analyze some of the incidents in which the Holy Spirit worked for the outreach of the church with the message of salvation.

Once again a word of caution is in order. It is always wise to keep in mind that the book of Acts is a narrative of what happened at a given time in the history of the early church. It is not a didactic book in the sense of being written to teach doctrine. It is historical rather than doctrinal in purpose. Therefore, we must not expect or demand that everything that happened in Acts is necessarily to be repeated in our experience today. Nevertheless, Acts does give us excellent examples of how the Spirit of God works in his people. So we can take its illustrations as a basis for understanding his methods.

Two of the most essential works of the Holy Spirit, the baptism and the filling of the Spirit, have already been discussed. Therefore, although both of these are abundantly illustrated in Acts, we will pass over consideration of them and move on to other aspects of his ministry related to the outreach of the church.

THE HOLY SPIRIT CHOOSES SOME MEN FOR SPECIAL TASKS/ Every Christian has been called by God to himself. This is inherent in salvation. Every Christian has also been commanded to be a witness. The Great Commission passages studied in chapter 4 are for all Christians. No one who wants to be honest with God can evade his responsibility to share his faith in Jesus Christ with other people.

However, there is a sense in which the Holy Spirit picks out certain men for specific tasks. In so doing he calls these men to move forward with a new outreach for the gospel. The best example of this in Acts is found in chapter 13.

The church in Antioch had received the gospel through the witness of believers who had been scattered by persecution:

> Now those who were scattered because of the persecution that arose over Stephen traveled as far as Phoenicia and Cyprus and Antioch, speaking the word to none except Jews. But there were some of them, men of Cyprus and Cyrene, who on coming to Antioch spoke to the Greeks also, preaching the Lord Jesus. And the hand of the Lord was with them, and a great number that believed turned to the Lord. (Acts 11:19-21)

As the church grew, the apostles in Jerusalem heard of it and sent Barnabas, a man "full of the Holy Spirit and of faith," to encourage and exhort them. Barnabas, on seeing how well the church was doing, rejoiced. He recognized, however, that the task was too big for him alone. So he traveled to Tarsus to persuade Saul to join him in the work at

Antioch. For the next year these two gifted men worked together with the Antioch church. It was in this city that the disciples were for the first time called "Christians" (Acts 11:25-26).

Then suddenly a startling thing happened. While the church was worshiping the Lord together, a word came from the Holy Spirit, "Set apart for me Barnabas and Saul for the work to which I have called them" (Acts 13:2). How could this be? The Holy Spirit was asking the church to give up its best leaders! That's not the way "missionary calls" are supposed to happen! We expect the youth to be "called," but not the top leaders! Who would continue the work in Antioch? The church was still young and vulnerable to the growing pains expected in early development. It needed strong leaders. And besides, Antioch was far from evangelized. Only one church existed there. Corruption, poverty and sin were still rampant. In fact, one early writer tells us that "all the great cities of the Roman Empire doubtlessly vied with each other in dissoluteness of morals, but in this the palm probably belongs to Antioch."[1] Thus, with a new church in the midst of a very corrupt city, how could the Holy Spirit ask the church to send out its two best leaders?

There is no record of arguments or opposition from the Christians in Antioch. Rather, as soon as the call came from the Holy Spirit, "after fasting and praying they laid their hands on them and sent

71

them off" (Acts 13:3). Thus, it was the church that sent them out. However, the next verse says, "So, being sent out by the Holy Spirit, they went down to Seleucia . . ." (Acts 13:4). This shows the basic and important principle that the Holy Spirit calls and sends *through the church.* Barnabas and Saul received this call in the context of church fellowship, in the act of worship and through the church as a body. When the Holy Spirit sent them out, he was sending them with the cooperation of the church of which they were a part.

In this day of independence and anti-church feeling on the part of some, it is well to remember that the Holy Spirit has chosen to work through, and not apart from, the church, which is the body of Christ.

THE HOLY SPIRIT GUIDES THE CHURCH IN OUTREACH/ The book of Acts is full of illustrations of how the Spirit guided the church in its daily life and witness.

The Spirit guides to individuals. There are frequent illustrations of this truth, so we will mention just a few. In Acts 8, Philip was in the midst of a thriving revival in Samaria, when the Lord told him to leave the city and go down to the Gaza road in the desert. He could easily have argued that it was hardly logical to leave a big city revival to jaunt off into the desert. But Philip obeyed without question. When he got there, the Spirit led him to the

Ethiopian eunuch, who was returning home from Jerusalem. Here was a man whose heart was prepared as he was reading the Scriptures. Of all passages in the Old Testament that would make a good starting point for presenting the gospel, he was reading perhaps the best—Isaiah 53. The result of the leading of the Spirit and the obedience of Philip was the conversion of the Ethiopian, who "went on his way rejoicing." The Coptic Church today claims that its spiritual ancestry can be traced back to this man.

In Acts 9, Ananias, a man of Damascus, was told by the Lord to go to Saul of Tarsus. Ananias had his doubts about doing this, knowing that Saul was a great persecutor of the church. Yet he obeyed under the promptings of the Spirit. The result was the entrance of Saul into the family of God. The impact of the work of this man, who became Paul the Apostle, cannot be calculated. The obedience of Ananias to the leading of the Spirit was a key in this vital event.

The Spirit guides to ethnic groups. In Acts 10, Peter had a strange vision whose meaning was obscure to him. He saw a sheet let down from heaven, a sheet filled with unclean animals that the Jews were prohibited from eating by levitical law. A voice told him to rise and eat. When he refused, the voice said, "What God has cleansed, you must not call common" (Acts 10:15). While Peter pondered the meaning of this, he was invited by visitors to go

73

to the household of Cornelius, a Gentile. As a good Jew, Peter would not have gone, except that the Spirit told him to do so "without hesitation." He went and found Cornelius and his household seeking God and ready to receive the message of Jesus Christ. Thus Peter was God's instrument for opening the door of faith to the Gentiles, who until that time had been excluded by the Jewish Christians from receiving salvation through Christ. So, while Peter preached just to one man and his household, he was actually reaching out to an entire ethnic group.

It is worthy of note that in all three cases just mentioned, the men involved would have preferred not to go where the Spirit told them to go. Philip no doubt would have wanted to stay in Samaria rather than go to the desert. Ananias specifically argued about going to Saul, the great persecutor. And Peter would have had nothing to do with Gentiles had he been left to his own leanings. But in each case the Spirit of God prodded these men into an outreach which resulted in a great spread of the gospel.

The Spirit guides to geographical locations. While the call of God is not primarily geographical, there are times when he clearly leads men to geographical areas. This is explicitly noted in the words of Christ in Acts 1:8, when he tells the disciples that they are to go to Jerusalem, all Judea, Samaria and the end of the earth.

A study of Acts 16:6-9 with a map in hand shows how the Spirit led in geographical ways. Paul and his companions had preached the gospel in "the region of Phrygia and Galatia," which was the eastern part of Asia Minor. Then they were "forbidden by the Holy Spirit to speak the word in Asia," which was the southern region. So they tried to go north into Bithynia, "but the Spirit of Jesus did not allow them." So they went west and arrived at Troas, a seaport. Here the Lord gave Paul a vision of a man of Macedonia saying, "Come over to Macedonia and help us," which Paul and his team took to indicate that "God had called us to preach the gospel to them." So they went across into Macedonia—the first Christian missionaries to Europe. This was a direct result of geographical leading by the Spirit.

The Spirit guides in intangible ways. There may be times when the Spirit of God guides a man through an inner conviction that he should or should not take a certain step. This was Paul's experience in Acts 19:21: "Now after these events Paul resolved in the Spirit to pass through Macedonia and Achaia and go to Jerusalem, saying, 'After I have been there, I must also see Rome.'" There is no apparent outward reason here for guidance. Rather there is an inner conviction that this is what he should do. Goodspeed translates this, "Paul, under the Spirit's guidance, resolved. . . ." C. H. Rieu translates it, "the Spirit moved Paul to plan. . . ."

The same thing is seen in Acts 20:22-23, where Paul says, "And now, behold, I am going to Jerusalem, bound in the Spirit, not knowing what shall befall me there; except that the Holy Spirit testifies to me in every city that imprisonment and afflictions await me." Even though danger lay ahead, Paul seemed to have an inner conviction that he must go to Jerusalem anyway. The New English Bible says, "And now . . . I am on my way to Jerusalem, under the constraint of the Spirit."

Some years ago my colleague Ernest Fowler and I determined to visit an Indian tribe in Colombia where we had reason to believe the gospel had not yet gone. We laid plans carefully for our trip. We packed our knapsacks, had our hammocks and other equipment in good order, had maps of the river and surrounding jungle area where these Indians lived, and had our travel plans checked out. On the morning of departure I rose early for my accustomed quiet time with the Lord. For some strange reason, as I went to prayer, I became obsessed with an overwhelming sense of restraint about the trip. I could not pray with any freedom about it. I opened the Word, but nothing I read seemed to fit my need at the moment. For nearly an hour I struggled with this problem, wondering what God was trying to say to me. All I could sense was an intangible feeling that we should not go.

I went to Ernest (who had spent that night in our home so we could leave together at an early hour) and asked how he felt about the trip. He had not experienced the same sense of restraint that seemed to bear down on me. But when I explained my feelings he said, "Well, let's pray about this together and see what God says." After breakfast and some further discussion and prayer, Ernest said with a quiet, settled conviction, "I don't think we should go. If God has placed this restraint in your heart, whatever may be the reason, I don't think we should violate it. We won't go."

Ernie was no mystic, yet he was a man who walked closely with God. I deeply respected his opinions. Together we came to the conclusion that we would not go. No further light was given, but we had peace about cancelling the trip.

Three years later he and I received an invitation from two Indian brothers of that tribe to spend a week with them to teach them the Scriptures. They had become Christians through the witness of Colombian believers, but they needed instruction in the Word. They were our point of contact to enter this tribe with the Word of God. Three years earlier, when we had planned our trip, these two men were not yet Christians, nor was anyone else in the tribe. We would have had no bridge, no entering wedge, to commend us to the people had we gone at that time. God, in his own way, hindered us from going until his time was ripe. The only guidance we had was an inner restraint, which we know came from the Holy Spirit.

THE HOLY SPIRIT TEACHES THE CHURCH FOR FURTHER OUTREACH/ Acts 15 records the story of the first church council, which was called by the elders in Jerusalem to discuss the question of non-Jews becoming Christians. Was it necessary for them to fulfill certain requirements of the Mosaic Law (such as circumcision) in order to become followers of Christ? After much discussion, including Peter's and Paul's descriptions of how God had brought Gentiles to faith in Christ through their witness, a decision was reached: It was not necessary for Gentiles to be circumcised in order to be saved.

As the apostles and elders summarized their conclusions, they wrote a letter to the churches and sent it out with some of the leading men. They explained their understanding of salvation for the Gentiles. They stated that it was the leading of the Holy Spirit that brought them to this understanding. "For it has seemed good to the Holy Spirit and to us to lay upon you no greater burden than these necessary things . . ." (Acts 15:28). This decision opened once and for all the understanding of the church that salvation in Christ is for all men and must be made known to all men. It was the leading of the Holy Spirit that opened their minds to this important truth, paving the way for a worldwide outreach with the gospel. This was a fulfillment of Christ's promise in John 16:13, "When the Spirit of truth comes, he will guide you into all the truth."

THE HOLY SPIRIT GIVES GIFTS TO THE CHURCH FOR OUTREACH/ The question of gifts will be considered separately in chapter 7, but this outline of the work of the Spirit in Acts would be incomplete without reference to this question. As we shall see later, the gifts of the Spirit are given for specific purposes which are directly related to the outreach of the church in gospel witness. This is abundantly illustrated in Acts, where most of the spiritual gifts described elsewhere in the New Testament are seen in practical ways in the life of the church.

As we have seen, it would be difficult to read the book of Acts even superficially without noticing the direct relationship of the Holy Spirit to the growth of the church. He comes upon the believers, calls them, sends them, guides them, leads them into all truth and gives them the necessary gifts so that the Word of God may spread to the end of the earth.

6

"ONE BODY
AND ONE
SPIRIT"

It was New Year's Eve. In Times Square, at Hollywood and Vine, and elsewhere across the land loud horns were being tuned up. Festive party-goers were readying their fireworks, gathering their confetti, uncorking the champagne and preparing to let out all the stops when the stroke of midnight sounded.

At the same hour, on the wide-open prairies of central Illinois, a large and diversified crowd had also gathered for celebration. Their festivities, however, would not be with the blowing of horns or the bursting of fireworks. Theirs would be a quiet and solemn celebration of the central event of history—the death of Jesus Christ. A fitting way for the older generation to spend New Year's Eve, perhaps, but hardly what one would expect of the swinging youth culture of today. Yet this group of over 12,000 at the University of Illinois at Urbana was composed of more than 11,000 students plus missionaries, professors, pastors and laymen. They were gathering for the final service of the ninth Inter-Varsity Missionary Convention, known popularly as "Urbana 70."

Sitting on the platform in the oval Assembly Hall I had opportunity that night to study that vast audience. It was as diverse a group as could be found anywhere. There were young men with beards, long hair and leather vests. There were young men with short hair, ties and sport coats. There were young women with jeans, sweatshirts and beads. There were young women with miniskirts and colorful leotards, and others with trim pantsuits or maxis. There were hoary-headed missionary statesmen in dark suits and white shirts. There were younger missionaries with colorful striped shirts and handsome blazers. There were elderly women with character etched into their faces from long years of overseas service for Christ. There were younger missionary women who could not be distinguished, had they been in Times Square that night, from well-dressed secretaries or career women from Fifth Avenue. There were Orientals and Latins, Africans and Afro-Americans, Europeans and Asians, Anglo-Saxons and Indians.

Following a biblical exposition by Canadian mis-

sionary Elwyn Davies, a quiet-spoken Anglican rec-
tor, the Reverend John Stott of All Souls Church
in London, stepped to the podium and explained
to the hushed audience the significance of the celebration that was about to take place. Then 250
students, precisely trained for their job, received
the trays of bread and wine and spread them quick-
ly and efficiently through that huge auditiorium.
In a matter of moments every one of the widely
diversified individuals received the elements which
commemorate the death of Christ. Long-haired
eighteen-year-old and white-haired missionary sat
side by side in thankful remembrance of the death
of Christ, "who has made us both one, and has
broken down the dividing wall . . . that he might
create in himself one new man in place of the two,
so making peace, and might reconcile us both to
God in one body through the cross . . ." (Eph.
2:14-16).

The sense of unity that permeated the entire hall
was found in the person of Christ, who was being
honored. When the last person had received the
elements, the last hymn had been sung and the
final benediction had been pronounced, the true
spirit of unity was openly demonstrated. Almost as
though on cue, and yet in a totally spontaneous
way, the entire audience burst out singing

We are one in the Spirit, we are one in the Lord,
We are one in the Spirit, we are one in the Lord,
And we pray that all unity may one day be

> *restored;*
> *And they'll know we are Christians by our love,*
> *by our love,*
> *Yes, they'll know we are Christians by our love!*

Some hands were raised in praise, others were clasped in love to one another, others were folded in quiet worship. But every person present that night was conscious of a unity that could be born only through the Holy Spirit.

Then slowly and reluctantly the crowd began to disperse. Some went out quietly to pray. Others went out to shouts and songs of joy. But all went out having been exhorted to become a part of what God was doing through his church in the spread of the gospel around the world. And, as from previous Urbana conventions, scores, hundreds, possibly thousands, would eventually be led by God to the uttermost parts of the earth with the message of salvation.

The prayer of our Lord in John 17:20-21 was being answered in a tangible way. "I do not pray for these only, but also for those who believe in me through their word, that they may all be one; even as thou, Father, art in me, and I in thee, that they also may be in us, so that the world may believe that thou hast sent me."

For our purposes here, the important thing to note is that Christ made a direct link between the unity of Christians and the belief of those whom they would try to lead to Christ. That is, the world

mission of the church and the unity of that church
go hand in hand. Bishop Lesslie Newbigin of South
India highlighted this when he said,

> *The Church's unity is the sign and the instru-*
> *ment of the salvation which Christ has wrought*
> *and whose end is the summing-up of all things in*
> *Christ.*
>
> *Insofar as the Church is disunited her life is a*
> *direct and public contradiction of the Gospel.*
> *. . . There is one Lord, one faith, one atoning*
> *act, and one baptism by which we are made par-*
> *ticipants in that atonement. Insofar as we, who*
> *share that faith and that baptism, prove our-*
> *selves unwilling or unable to agree together in*
> *one fellowship, we publicly proclaim our dis-*
> *belief in the sufficiency of that atonement. No*
> *one who has shared in the task of seeking to*
> *commend Christ to those of other faiths can*
> *escape the shame of that denial.*[1]

The evangelistic task of the church is the area
where unity, or disunity, can best be seen. Where
the church is united, world mission can go forward;
where it is disunited, world mission suffers accordingly. Newbigin goes on to say,

> *Evangelistic work places the Church in a situa-*
> *tion in which the stark contrast between Christ*
> *and no-Christ is constantly being faced. In such*
> *a situation other matters necessarily fall into*
> *second place . . . I do not think that a resolute*
> *dealing with our divisions will come except in*

*the context of a quite new acceptance on the
part of all the Churches of the obligation to
bring the Gospel to every creature.*[2]

My wife and I lived for nine years in Cartagena,
Colombia, a city where cooperation between the
few small evangelical churches that existed there
was fragmentary at best. While the church in the
surrounding rural areas was alive and growing, very
little church growth, evangelistic zeal or unity was
experienced in that city. Several years after leaving
there, I had the opportunity to return for a brief
weekend visit. That Sunday all the churches in the
city were cooperating in launching a city-wide
evangelistic campaign to be held in the municipal
sports stadium for the next six weeks.

On Saturday night prior to the campaign the
churches joined in a marathon five hour prayer
meeting. Hundreds of people jammed to over-
flowing a church which, in other years, would have
considered itself fortunate if a couple of dozen believers showed up for such a meeting. Throughout
the evening they sang, read Scripture and prayed,
as different churches took turns leading the service.
One song which they sang repeatedly throughout
the night with great enthusiasm went like this:

*No me importa la iglesia a que vayas
Si detrás del Calvario tu estás;
Si tu corazón es como el mio
Dame la mano y mi hermano serás.*

The gist of this song is: "It makes no difference to

me what church you attend, if you stand behind
Calvary. If your heart is like mine, give me your
hand, and you're my brother." As they sang this
over and over (often repeating it five or six times in
a row), they would move around the church, up
and down the aisles and pews, extending their
hands to one another or embracing one another in
an expression of brotherly love in Christ. This
sense of oneness in Christ was coming not so much
through a theological recognition of the unity of
the body of Christ (something which they had
known in their heads for years), but rather through
an acceptance of their mutual obligations to make
the gospel known to their entire city. Unity was
being realized in mission, and mission brought
unity.

This is the work of the Holy Spirit in answer to
that prayer of Christ in John 17. The Spirit unites
the body of Christ "so that the world may believe."

One of the things which the Holy Spirit does in
order that the world may believe is to give gifts to
the church. These will be discussed in more detail
in the next chapter. But it must be noted here that
in every major passage where these gifts are explained, the unity of the body of Christ is the
setting in which they are discussed. Notice the
emphasis on unity which lays the foundation for
the diversity of gifts in the following passages.

For as in one body we have many members, and

all the members do not have the same function, so we, though many, are one body in Christ, and individually members one of another. Having gifts that differ according to the grace given to us, let us use them. . . . (Rom. 12:4-6)

Now there are varieties of gifts, but the same Spirit; and there are varieties of service, but the same Lord; and there are varieties of working, but it is the same God who inspires them all in every one. . . . For just as the body is one and has many members, and all the members of the body, though many, are one body, so it is with Christ. . . . For the body does not consist of one member but of many. (1 Cor. 12:4-6, 12, 14)

There is one body and one Spirit, just as you were called to the one hope that belongs to your call, one Lord, one faith, one baptism, one God and Father of us all. . . . But grace was given to each of us according to the measure of Christ's gift. Therefore it is said, "When he ascended on high he led a host of captives, and he gave gifts to men." (Eph. 4:4-8)

As the Spirit binds the church together as one body and gives gifts for the edification of that body and its outreach to others, several things result.

First, there is a recognition of the fact that we are all members of the same body. It is this concept which brings forth the spontaneous singing of "We Are One in the Spirit," as enthusiastic young people, and older ones as well, realize what God has done for them.

Second, there is a recognition of the great task which Christ has given to his body, namely, to make the good news of his salvation known throughout the world. Writing to the same Corinthians to whom he had explained the concept of the body, Paul says that God, in reconciling the world to himself through Christ, is "entrusting to us the ministry of reconciliation. So we are ambassadors for Christ, God making his appeal through us" (2 Cor. 5:19). That is, the task of making known the message of reconciliation through Christ has been placed in our hands. It is the same task for all believers. Thus, when the churches in Cartagena began to take this seriously, a unity developed which had never before been experienced.

This same truth is being seen today around the world in nationwide programs of total mobilization for evangelism. Such movements as Evangelism-in-Depth in Latin America, New Life for All in Africa and saturation evangelism efforts in Asia have taken as one key foundation stone the unity of the body of Christ in reaching the world for him.

Third, the varieties of gifts, of service and of ways of working (compare 1 Cor. 12:4-6) are recognized as legitimate outworkings of that unity. When the body is aware of its essential unity, it can then accept and utilize the greatly diversified gifts which the Spirit gives to its members. Instead of becoming suspicious of another person whose method may differ from mine, I can accept him as a fellow member of the body who has been gifted in a different way than I to accomplish God's purposes. Instead of becoming insecure and worried about my own place in the body, I can rejoice with him in his gifts and strive to use mine in conjunction with his for the glory of God.

Barnabas gives us one of the best New Testament illustrations of this. When a new church was growing up in Antioch, the apostles in Jerusalem sent Barnabas (whose name, meaning "Son of Encouragement," indicates what his gifts were) to assist and encourage the new believers. "When he came and saw the grace of God, he was glad; and he exhorted them all to remain faithful to the Lord with steadfast purpose" (Acts 11:23).

Then, realizing that his particular gifts could be supplemented by a young man whose gifts were different and perhaps more extensive than his own, Barnabas traveled to Tarsus and persuaded Saul to come to Antioch to help him develop the church there. In so doing Barnabas was risking his own future fame. He was bringing onto the scene a man whose gifts were destined to overshadow his own. Barnabas would soon recede quietly into a place of less fame and public exposure. He, no doubt, knew this when he went to Tarsus to get Saul. But he had one great desire, and that was that the believers in Antioch should get all the help they could in growing in grace. So he did not hesitate to bring into the picture a man more gifted than himself.

This recognition of the diversity of gifts within the unity of the body is a key to world mission. As the Holy Spirit unites the body, he also gives gifts within the body. The purpose and scope of these gifts as they relate to world evangelism must now be studied in closer detail.

7

"VARIETIES
OF GIFTS BUT
THE SAME SPIRIT"

Cartagena, Colombia, is an ancient seaport built by the Spaniards in 1534. It originally served as a center for shipping the gold taken from the Inca Empire to Spain. As such, it frequently came under attack from pirates. So from its earliest days the city was surrounded by sturdy walls. A massive fort, largest in the western hemisphere, stands guard over the city, aided by several smaller forts strategically located near the entrance to the harbor. So thick are the city walls that it is possible in some places for cars to drive several abreast on top of the walls.

One day I drove a pickup truck filled with ten believers from the backwoods of Colombia up on top of those walls to look out over the sparkling blue Caribbean Sea. For some of them it was their first visit to a city of this size. Some had never seen the ocean before, having lived all their lives in jungles or rural farming areas. It was a revealing experience to note their reactions. One man, seeing the walls for the first time, commented, "So that's what a walled city looks like! That must be what Jericho looked like."

As we drove along on top of the walls, he said, "Wasn't it Nineveh where chariots could ride six abreast on top of the walls? So this must be like Nineveh!"

As they stood contemplating the vast expanse of ocean stretching unbroken out to the distant horizon, one man commented, "Imagine the faith it would take to walk on water like that!" Then, watching the waves crashing against the rocks on shore, he added, "And just imagine the power it would take to speak to those waves and tell them to be still and then see them obey!"

Why were they reacting in this way? Because they were men and women who were saturated with the Scripture. Some of them could not read. Others could read only with difficulty. But their entire lives revolved around the Word of God, as they read it for themselves at every opportunity or listened to others who could read it to them. Thus when they saw something new or encountered a new experience, their most natural reaction was to compare what they were seeing with Bible stories of something similar.

This saturation in the Scriptures was also the reason for their visit to Cartagena. As they dug into the Word, they had begun to understand something of the spiritual gifts given to the church by the Holy Spirit. Soon they began to experience these gifts in their midst. As they received some gifts and studied them in the light of God's Word, they came to understand several great truths. Each person was to receive some gift from the Lord. Some are given to one person, others to another person. Not all have the same gifts. Also they saw that these were to be used for the common good of the church for its outreach.

As spiritual gifts became evident among them, they came to the conclusion that these should not be kept to themselves but should be exercised for the good of others. So they developed what they called "La Campaña"—"The Campaign." This was a group of ten believers formed into a team based on spiritual gifts. The team traveled around from village to village, and then from city to city, for the purpose of using their gifts on behalf of others. One man had the gift of preaching, so he would exhort the church. Another had the gift of evangelism, and he would be used in this way. Another had the gift of faith, so he led them in their prayer ministry. Sometimes he and others would pray all during a service as another team member was preaching. Another had the gift of healing and used

95

it with the prayer backing of the others. Several had the gift of tongues, and one had the gift of interpretation to accompany it. One woman had the gift of helps and used it constantly in the service of others.

These men and women had come to Cartagena to minister to the churches of that city, sharing their own faith through the exercise of God-given gifts.

What were the gifts they experienced, and what does the New Testament say about them? Three major passages discuss the question of gifts: Romans 12, 1 Corinthians 12 and Ephesians 4. While some outstanding writers and preachers refer to the "nine gifts" of the Spirit (probably because there are nine that appear in 1 Corinthians 12), it seems doubtful that Paul was trying to be exhaustive in any or in all of the lists he gives. Rather, it is more likely that Paul was giving examples of what the Spirit does for individuals in equipping them to do his work. In so doing he refers to specific gifts.

There are various possible classifications for these gifts, such as "gifts which qualify their possessors for the ministry of the Word, . . . gifts which equip their possessors to render services of a practical nature";[1] "spiritual gifts for preaching and teaching; prophetical ministry; spiritual gifts of action";[2] "non-remarkable and remarkable";[3] "men given to the church; gifts given to men"; "natural

and supernatural"—to name a few of the possibilities.

MEANING OF THE WORD GIFT/ There are
nine different Greek words translated as "gift" in
our English versions. However, the one that most
concerns this study is the word *charisma,* since this
is employed in Romans 12 and 1 Corinthians 12 in
discussing spiritual gifts. Arndt and Gingrich define
charisma as "a gift (freely and graciously given), a
favor bestowed." They also give it the meaning of
"special gifts of a non-material sort, bestowed by
the grace of God on individual Christians . . . of
spiritual gifts in a special sense."[4] It is from this
word, of course, that our English word *charismatic*
is taken.

In Ephesians 4:7-8, Paul employs two words to
refer to gifts, *dorea* and *doma,* both of which can
be translated simply as "gift," meaning something
freely given.[5]

LIST OF THE GIFTS/ On the following page is
a list of the gifts mentioned in the major passages,
one which makes no attempt at classifying or com-
bining them into a set number, but, rather, just
notes where they occur.

It is quite possible that some of these gifts are
called by one name in one place and another name
in another passage. For example, "he who gives
aid" (Rom. 12:8) and "helpers" (1 Cor. 12:28)

Gift	Rom. 12	1 Cor. 12	Eph. 4
Prophecy	X	X	X
Service	X		
Teaching	X	X	X
Exhorting	X		
Contributing	X		
Giving aid	X		
Acts of mercy	X		
Utterance of wisdom		X	
Utterance of knowledge		X	
Faith		X	
Healing		X	
Miracles		X	
Discerning of spirits		X	
Tongues		X	
Interpretation of tongues		X	
Apostles		X	X
Helpers		X	
Administrators		X	
Evangelists			X
Pastors			X

may well be the same gift. It should also be noted that 1 Peter 4:10-11 refers to gifts in a general way, mentioning specifically "whoever speaks" and "whoever renders service."

SOURCE OF THE GIFTS/ Each of the three major passages makes clear where the gifts originate. In fact, it is interesting to observe that each of the three members of the Trinity is mentioned as the source of the gifts. In Romans 12, Paul exhorts each one "not to think of himself more highly than he ought to think, but to think with sober judgment, each according to the measure of faith which God has assigned him" (Rom. 12:3). Then he moves directly on to say, "Having gifts that differ according to the grace given to us, let us use them . . ." (v. 6). The context makes clear that the gifts are given by God, who gives the measure of faith.

In 1 Corinthians 12, Paul speaks of the Spirit as the source of the gifts: "To each is given the manifestation of the Spirit for the common good. To one is given through the Spirit the utterance of wisdom, and to another the utterance of knowledge [etc.]. . . . All these are inspired by one and the same Spirit, who apportions to each one individually as he wills" (vv. 7-8, 11).

In Ephesians, Paul speaks of Christ as giving gifts: "But grace was given to each of us according to the measure of Christ's gift. Therefore it is said,

'When he ascended on high he led a host of captives, and he gave gifts to men.' . . . And his gifts were that some should be apostles [etc.] . . ." (Eph. 4:7-8, 11).

Since God, with his Son and with his Spirit, is the giver of the gifts, it must also be noted that the gifts are given "as he wills" (1 Cor. 12:11). It is a sovereign act of God through his Spirit to give gifts. He gives them to whom he wills. That is, he knows who needs what gifts, and he apportions them accordingly. Therefore, we receive our gifts on the basis of his will, not ours. I may wish for a particular gift, I may pray earnestly for it, but God knows which gifts I need. He will impart to me what he wants me to have.

SCOPE OF THE GIFTS/ Gifts are given to every believer: "To each is given the manifestation of the Spirit for the common good. . . . All these are inspired by one and the same Spirit, who apportions to each one individually as he wills" (1 Cor. 12:7, 11). While not every believer has every gift (in fact, it may be questioned if *any* believer has *every* gift), every Christian is given some gift by the Spirit.

The scope of these gifts is broad; they reach into every area of life. "I give thanks to God always for you because of the grace of God which was given you in Christ Jesus, that *in every way* you were enriched in him with all speech and all knowledge

—even as the testimony to Christ was confirmed among you—so that you are not lacking in any spiritual gift, as you wait for the revealing of our Lord Jesus Christ" (1 Cor. 1:4-7). In other words, the spiritual gifts are to enrich us in every way, and all the gifts needed for that enrichment will be given.

PURPOSE OF THE GIFTS/   In Ephesians 4, Paul gives the clearest explanation of why God gives gifts to his church. The New English Bible translates it this way: "And these were his gifts: some to be apostles, some prophets, some evangelists, some pastors and teachers, to equip God's people for work in his service, to the building up of the body of Christ" (Eph. 4:11-12). The Living Bible paraphrases Ephesians 4:12 this way: "Why is it that he gives us these special abilities to do certain things best? It is that God's people will be equipped to do better work for him, building up the church, the body of Christ, to a position of strength and maturity." Thus the purpose of the gifts is to equip the individual Christian so that he can participate effectively in building up the whole church. This immediately destroys the artifical gap between "clergy" and "laity." God has not called a spiritual elite to carry out the work of the ministry, by-passing the ordinary believer in the church. Rather, "*to each* is given the manifestation of the Spirit for the common good" (1 Cor. 12:7).

It is true that some are called to positions of more prominence, in a public sense, than others. The gifts of apostle, prophet, evangelist, pastor and teacher will inevitably place those individuals who have them in a more noticeable position than the ones who have gifts of helps, mercy or giving liberally. But God does not set up a spiritual hierarchy whereby some are more important in his eyes than others. Rather, God looks for faithfulness in using what he has given us.

The parable of the talents (Mt. 25:14-30) bears mentioning here. The master who parcelled out talents to his servants expected a just accounting when he returned. He expected the one who received five talents to account for them adequately. Likewise the ones who received two and one talent were expected to give an account. From the one to whom he had given one talent, he did not expect five in return. He only expected one more in return, but he did expect that one. To those servants who had faithfully invested what he had given them, he said, "Well done, good and faithful servant; you have been faithful over a little, I will set you over much; enter into the joy of your master." But to the one who had hoarded the one talent he had received, the master said, "You wicked and slothful servant!" and he took from him the one talent he had buried.

This bears out the emphasis in 1 Corinthians 12:7 that the gifts are given *for the common good.*

They are not to be kept selfishly or buried in the
ground but rather to be shared with the whole
body of Christ. This was one of the truths which
my friends in The Campaign had perceived. They
had been given a variety of gifts, and they wished
to share them for the common good of the church,
each one supplementing and supporting the others.

Another purpose of the gifts is to unite, not to
divide, the body of Christ. In all three passages
where gifts are discussed, the unity of Christians is
emphasized, as we have noted in the previous chapter. In Romans, Paul says: "For as in *one body*
we have many members, and all the members
do not have the same function, so we, though
many, are *one body in Christ,* and individually
members one of another. Having gifts that differ
according to the grace given to us, let us use them"
(Rom. 12:4-6). In the Corinthians passage, the oneness of the body forms the entire context in which
gifts are considered.

> *Now there are varieties of gifts, but* the same
> Spirit; *and there are varieties of service, but* the
> same Lord; *and there are varieties of working,
> but it is* the same God *who inspires them all in
> every one. . . . For just as* the body is one *and
> has many members, and all the members of the
> body, though many, are* one body, *so it is with
> Christ. For by* one Spirit *we were all baptized
> into one body—Jews or Greeks, slaves or free—
> and all were made to drink of* one Spirit. *. . . But*

God has so adjusted the body, giving the greater honor to the inferior part, that there may be no discord in the body, *but that the members may have the same care for one another. . . . Now you are the body of Christ and individually members of it. (1 Cor. 12:4-6, 12-13, 24-25, 27)*

In Ephesians, as he prepares to speak of the gifts, Paul says that he is "eager to maintain *the unity of the Spirit* in the bond of peace. There is *one body* and *one Spirit,* just as you were called to the *one hope* that belongs to your call, *one Lord, one faith, one baptism, one God and Father* of us all. . . . But grace was given to each of us according to the measure of Christ's gift" (Eph. 4:3-7).

It is impossible to read these passages even superficially and miss the emphasis on the oneness of the body of Christ and how the gifts are to contribute to this unity. Therefore, when gifts in the church serve to divide rather than to unite, we can be sure that one of two things has occurred: Either what is being exercised is not a true gift from God, or a true gift from God is being used in an unscriptural way.

One of the most tragic sights in all of Christendom is a church torn apart by dissension over the gifts of the Spirit. Some will naively contend that any supernatural or remarkable outward manifestation of power (be it tongues, healing, miracles or something similar) must be evidence of the power of the Spirit. Yet Christ himself warned, "For false

Christs and false prophets will arise and show great signs and wonders, so as to lead astray, if possible, even the elect" (Mt. 24:24). He also spoke of those who in the day of judgment will say, "Lord, Lord, did we not prophesy in your name, and cast out demons in your name, and do many mighty works in your name? And then will I declare to them, I never knew you; depart from me, you evildoers" (Mt. 7:22-23).

Therefore, the mere manifestation of something beyond normal human powers is no guarantee of the power of the Spirit in one's life. It may be satanic power or in some cases a psychological reaction which produces an apparent "sign." But if it divides Christians, it is not in accord with the purposes for which the gifts of the Spirit are given. When true gifts are exercised in a biblical way, there will be a oneness of spirit in the body. And then the prayer of Christ will be answered, "that they all may be one . . . so that the world may believe that thou hast sent me" (Jn. 17:21). This unity of the body will result in outreach to others, that they too may believe.

This relationship of the gifts of the Spirit to the worldwide outreach of the church is well expressed by a leading writer of the Pentecostal persuasion, the Reverend Donald Gee:

> Therefore we must hold fast to rightly understanding the gifts of the Spirit as a divine equipment for the work of World Evangelization. To

regard them in any other way is to turn them into a specialty for groups of people that become little more than religious clubs. Particularly is this so when there is an over-emphasis upon "messages" through prophetical gifts, and still more if it is by means of Tongues and Interpretation of Tongues. They possess a strange fascination when first encountered that tends to sweep novices off their feet. There is NO future for gifts of the Spirit on that line, except in the stagnant backwaters of an esoteric sect. When the element of novelty wears off, which is inevitable, it leaves the devotees isolated from the main stream of healthy evangelical Christianity. This has happened, is happening, and will happen again if we do not keep balanced and sane in our appreciation of spiritual gifts. They are not a hobby to play with; they are tools to work with and weapons to fight with.[6]

8

"TONGUES OF MEN AND OF ANGELS"

The sounds of the surrounding forest that night were no different from any other night: the rustle of leaves in the towering bongo and eucalyptus trees, the call of an occasional bird of the night, the chirps of crickets, the patter of a lizard scampering up the bamboo wall. Juan Gonzalez, a young man in his late teens who had recently become a Christian, was praying alone in his house. As was the custom of believers in rural Colombia he prayed aloud, although he was alone. His opportunity for education had been so limited that he barely knew how to read and write. Thus his knowledge of the Bible was as yet very elemental. His heart was warmed with praise to God as he expressed his gratitude and love to the Lord whom he had recently met.

Suddenly, without warning of any sort, Juan became aware of the most confusing thing he had ever experienced. While the sounds of the forest had not changed, the sounds coming from his mouth had! His expression of praise to God had abruptly become unintelligible to him. Although he was conscious that he was continuing to pray, it was not Spanish (his mother tongue) that was coming out. It was some other language! Yet he knew in his heart that he was still speaking to God. He was experiencing a phenomenon which he had never heard of and for which he could find no explanation.

Confused and frightened, Juan went the next day to Victor Landero, his spiritual father and the leader of the Christians in his area. Neither Victor nor Juan had ever met a Pentecostal nor had they heard anything about charismatic gifts. Thus Juan's experience of expressing himself to God in an unintelligible tongue was totally new to them. Although Victor was still a relatively new Christian himself and knew the Scriptures only through his own study and reading, he remembered that the book of Acts spoke about such a phenomenon. Therefore, Victor began an intensive study of Acts to try to figure out what this strange experience signified. Each week he led the Christians in the little village of Corozalito, where he lived, in a study of Acts, trying to keep ahead of them in his own studies.

Two weeks later Victor experienced the same phenomenon, except in his case he experienced it in public. He was leading in prayer in a meeting, when suddenly he found himself praying in an unfamiliar language. As in Juan's case, Victor was quite conscious that he was still praying to God, even though he could not understand what was being expressed. He had a strong sense of praise and worship welling up from his heart.

During the next months and years the question of tongues became the focal point around which everything else seemed to revolve. Many wanted to receive the gift and took every step possible to work it up. Others were repelled by it and took extreme positions against it. As so often happens in connection with this particular gift, the churches were soon dividing up into two camps: those who felt that tongues was a sign which every believer had to experience as an indication of his baptism in the Holy Spirit and those who felt it was either of the devil or at least of the flesh and was to be avoided at all costs.

As missionaries working with the church in that region, my colleagues and I found ourselves caught in a crossfire. We tried to be open to all that the Spirit of God was doing, including giving miraculous gifts. We did not want to be guilty of quenching the Spirit. At the same time we tried to find a scriptural balance and put this gift into its proper perspective. In the process we were attacked from all sides. Some of the more extreme charismatic brethren accused us of being anti-Holy Spirit because we did not speak in tongues. Extremists on the other side accused us of turning Pentecostal because we were open to what we felt the Spirit was trying to do. Still others accused us of vacillating in the middle, not knowing what we believed.

In the heat of the battle over this issue, which raged for several years, I found great help from Christ's statement to the Sadducees, "You are wrong, because you know neither the scriptures nor the power of God" (Mt. 22:29). Error on either of these points results in faulty doctrine and erroneous experience. One must understand first and foremost what the Scriptures teach. This is the foundation rock of all our understanding of God and his ways with us. At the same time the truths of Scripture must be experienced in the life of the individual. His power must be manifest in an experiential way, or the truths of Scripture are meaningless. The holy life became the object of our quest. The pages that follow will attempt to express the understanding that grew out of this controversy. What do the Scriptures say? How can the power of God be manifest in daily life? These two touchstones became crucial in our understanding of this delicate subject.

WHAT IS THE GIFT OF TONGUES?/ The

Greek word employed for "tongues" is *glossa,*
from which we get our word *glossalalia,* referring
to the experience of speaking in an unknown language. *Glossa* can mean the organ of the tongue or
the language which proceeds from the tongue.
Luke uses this word in Acts 2:4, saying that the
Christians on the day of Pentecost, when the Holy
Spirit came upon them, spoke in "other tongues."
These were languages, for we read that men "from
every nation under heaven" were present in Jerusalem that day and heard the message in their own
language.

In 1 Corinthians 12—14, Paul also employs
glossa to refer to the spiritual experience of expressing oneself to God in words unknown to the
one who is speaking. Modern day linguists have
studied such tongues scientifically. Many have concluded that generally such utterances are in no
known human language.[1]

In considering what this gift really is, it will help
to look at it first negatively and then positively.

Negatively, *what the gift is not.* First, it is not
the evidence of the baptism of the Holy Spirit. If
we accept the thesis of chapter 2, that the baptism
of the Spirit is that which takes place at the moment of conversion, then there is no scriptural
grounds for claiming that tongues must be the sign
of that baptism. We look in vain in the Bible for
any indication that every time a person comes to
Christ he must also speak in tongues. In fact, quite

111

the opposite is true. It was a rare occasion in Acts, for example, when these two things went hand in hand in the experience of Christians. Never in the teachings of Christ and the apostles are they combined as contiguous.

Second, the gift of tongues is not the evidence of the fullness of the Holy Spirit. Again, the Scriptures nowhere indicate that these two things will accompany one another. Admittedly they sometimes do. But there is no teaching in any part of the New Testament which makes this a necessary conjunction. Rather, the contrary is true. In Acts there are nine cases where individuals or groups were filled with the Spirit. In only one of these did they speak in tongues (Acts 2). I am aware that there are three cases of tongues in Acts, but on two of those occasions it does not specifically say that they were filled with the Spirit, although presumably they were. It is well to note, however, that on eight separate occasions the fullness of the Spirit was not accompanied by tongues.

When Paul commanded the Ephesians to "be filled with the Spirit" (Eph. 5:18), he went on to exhort them to continue "addressing one another in psalms and hymns and spiritual songs, singing and making melody to the Lord with all your heart, always and for everything giving thanks in the name of our Lord Jesus Christ to God the Father" (Eph. 5:19-20). But no mention is made of speaking in tongues as though it were to be expected as an accompanying sign to that fullness they were to seek.

Making tongues a sign of some post-conversion spiritual experience is unwarranted in the Bible and can lead, unfortunately, to an unbalanced view of what the Christian life is all about. In discussing tongues as a sign of the fullness or baptism of the Holy Spirit, Bruner highlights this when he says,

> But the moment any rite, any obedience, any experience, no matter how buttressed with Scripture or with "angels from heaven," becomes a supplement to faith or a condition for fulness before God, then the anathema must be announced and the warning to avoid false teaching urged with all possible seriousness. . . . The supplement to faith seems historically destined to become the center of a new faith. . . . It appears to be historically true that every supplement to faith has within itself the almost irresistible tendency of becoming eventually a specific advancement beyond faith and thus to become inevitably the goal of a new spirituality of a purportedly higher Christian type. Faith itself then becomes but a step in the right direction. In a word, the supplement "and" is pregnant with the ineluctable tendency to become the central "more."[2]

Positively, *what the gift is*. The gift of tongues is that which enables a person to express something (such as praise and worship to God, or a prophetic

113

message from God through interpretation) in a language which he has not learned. Whether this is a known human language or merely an ecstatic utterance of an unknown tongue is an issue which is debated on both sides. In Acts 2, it certainly appears that the disciples were speaking known languages, since the language groups are specified by name, such as "Parthians and Medes and Elamites and residents of Mesopotamia, Judea and Cappadocia, Pontus and Asia" (Acts 2:9-11). These people testified, "We hear them telling in our own tongues the mighty works of God" (Acts 2:11).

Some will contend that the miracle was not in the speaking but in the hearing. That is, the disciples were only speaking their own language, but the men from other countries were hearing the message in their own tongues. Not much is gained by assuming this, since it still requires a miraculous intervention of God to produce such an impression. It would seem to fit the context more fully to accept this as a genuine case in which known languages were spoken. In fact, Luke's use of the phrase "other tongues" (Acts 2:4) confirms this. Before unbelievers heard them, they were already speaking in "other tongues," indicating that the miracle was not in the hearing but in the disciples' speaking tongues which were not their own language.

Some Bible scholars believe that since the same word, *glossa,* is used in Acts and in 1 Corinthians

12—14, this indicates that tongues are always known languages. But J. Oswald Sanders has pointed out numerous differences between the gift of tongues in Acts 2 and the gift as mentioned in 1 Corinthians 12—14. He says,

> While there may be some correspondences, there are strong contrasts between the tongues-speaking at Pentecost and that at Corinth.
> At Pentecost all *spoke in tongues (Acts 2:4).*
> This was not true of the believers at Corinth (1 Cor. 12:30).
> At Pentecost the tongues were understood by all (Acts 2:6).
> At Corinth they were understood by none (1 Cor. 14:2).
> At Pentecost they spoke to men (Acts 2:6).
> At Corinth they spoke to God (1 Cor. 14:2, 9).
> At Pentecost no interpreter was necessary (Acts 2:6).
> At Corinth tongues-speaking was forbidden if no interpreter was present (1 Cor. 14:23, 28).
> At Pentecost tongues were a sign or credential to believers (Acts 11:15).
> At Corinth it was a sign to unbelievers (1 Cor. 14:22).
> At Pentecost strangers were filled with awe and marvelled (Acts 2:7-8).
> At Corinth Paul warned that strangers would say they were mad (1 Cor. 14:23).
> At Pentecost there was perfect harmony (Acts

2:1).

At Corinth there was confusion (1 Cor. 14:33).[3]

Sanders concludes that "since there is such a marked difference, between these two manifestations of the gift of tongues, it would not be sound exegesis to build a system of doctrine on the identity of the two occurrences."[4]

It would appear, then, as is so often the case, that the truth lies between the extremes of saying that all tongues are known languages or that no tongues are known languages. If God chose to give known languages on the day of Pentecost, who are we to claim that he cannot do it again? On the other hand, the whole context of the Corinthian experience seems to indicate that the tongues being used there were ecstatic utterances that did not fit any known language pattern. Paul speaks of them as "various kinds of tongues" (1 Cor. 12:10), indicating that they will differ. In 1 Corinthians 14:10-11, Paul speaks of "many different languages in the world." Here he uses not the word *glossa* but rather the word *phone.*

It would appear that, in this context, Paul has introduced the word *phone,* meaning known languages, to contrast it with *glossa,* meaning ecstatic utterances of unknown tongues. *Glossa* can, of course, mean known languages, as it did in Acts 2. However, in the context of 1 Corinthians 14 it seems that Paul is referring to utterances which are not in the language of the speaker and may not be

any known human language. This would agree with
the studies of the linguists who indicate that today's glossalalia seldom if ever fit any known language.

It is also possible that God may give today the
ability to speak in a language unknown to the
speaker but known to the hearer, as he did on the
day of Pentecost. A friend of mine, a missionary
from Australia in Colombia, has shared with me
how God once caused him to speak in a language
he had not learned. He was traveling on a train in
Australia and was seated next to a young Arab. He
had a desire to witness to the man about Christ,
but no opportunity opened up in their conversation. Apparently the Arab's English was limited.
Suddenly my friend found himself speaking in a
language which was unintelligible to him. This continued for about fifteen minutes while the Arab
listened intently.

When he finished the young man said, "Where
did you learn such perfect Arabic?"

My friend replied, "I never learned Arabic."

"Well, you just spoke to me in perfect Arabic
for fifteen minutes."

"What did I say?"

Whereupon the young Arab reviewed what had
been said, outlining the entire message of the
gospel! My friend says that this never happened
before or since in his experience.

Before leaving this section, we should note that there are three possible types of tongues. First, there is the genuine gift given by the Holy Spirit. This is what we are discussing here.

Second, there is a satanic imitation of that gift. Christ warned that Satan will produce "false Christs and false prophets" who will "show great signs and wonders" (Mt. 24:24). This can include speaking in tongues. This "gift" is practiced at times among Muslims, Buddhists, Hindus and others who do not have the Spirit of God dwelling in them. Where does it come from? Certainly not from the Spirit of God.

Third, there is a humanly produced psychological reaction that may result in supposed "tongues." A person who strives hard enough to produce an outward manifestation of tongues may succeed. But this does not mean that the noises which emit from his mouth are necessarily a gift from the Holy Spirit.

I talked with a student friend of mine in Pennsylvania who claimed he had received the gift of tongues. When I asked him to describe his experience, the following conversation ensued:

"I went to the church one evening and began to pray at the altar. I prayed from 8:00 p.m. to 2:00 a.m."

"What did you say for those six hours?"

"I said, 'Thank you, Jesus! Thank you, Jesus! Thank you, Jesus!' "

"For six hours?"

"Yes. Then at 2:00 a.m. the Holy Spirit grabbed hold of my jaw, and I lost control of it, and before I knew it, I was speaking in tongues."

My reaction to this was that anyone who said the same three words over and over and over for six hours might well lose control of his jaw and start babbling unintelligible words. While I believe in the gift of tongues, I do not believe that this student had received it on that occasion. He had experienced a psychological or even physiological reaction which was neither from the Spirit nor from Satan.

WHAT IS THE PURPOSE OF THE GIFT OF TONGUES?/ On the day of Pentecost the purpose of the gift of tongues was clear. First, it was a sign to the disciples that the Holy Spirit, promised by Christ just before his ascension, had now come in power. Had they received no outward manifestation, there could have been prolonged arguments about whether or not the Comforter had really come. The gift of tongues eliminated any doubt from their minds.

Second, it was to enable the Jewish proselytes in Jerusalem on that day to hear the message of salvation in their own languages. While many of them no doubt understood Greek or Aramaic, they unquestionably understood God's message better when it came through in their own tongue.

119

Paul gives four other reasons for or results of the gift of tongues in his discourse in 1 Corinthians 14:

1. It is for speaking to God in worship and praise. "For one who speaks in a tongue speaks not to men but to God" (v. 2).

2. It can produce personal edification. "He who speaks in a tongue edifies himself" (v. 4).

3. It can edify the church when used with an interpreter. "Let all things be done for edification. If any speak in a tongue, let there be only two or at most three . . . and let one interpret" (vv. 26-27).

4. It may be a sign to unbelievers. "Thus, tongues are a sign not for believers but for unbelievers" (v. 22).

Donald Gee emphasizes the devotional character of tongues, stating that it is primarily (although not exclusively) for private rather than public use.

The context teaches that the purpose of the Gift of Tongues is devotional, and for uttering praise or prayer. It is a language given to the human spirit by the Holy Spirit for expressing ecstatic utterances that the speaker finds it difficult to declare in his ordinary language. Obviously this would not be of use in a public meeting where no man could understand it, and for that purpose the Spirit can give a parallel gift of "Interpretation of Tongues" in order that others may be able to say an intelligent "Amen." This does not alter the essentially devotional character of

*the utterance in a "Tongue," nor turn it into a
message. We are left with the plain inference
that the proper sphere for the Gift of Tongues is
in private devotion, and for that reason it need
not occupy us unduly as a Gift for ministry.*[5]

WHO RECEIVES THE GIFT OF TONGUES?/ 1
Corinthians 12 and 14 make it clear that some receive this gift, others do not. "To one is given
through the Spirit . . . various kinds of tongues, to
another the interpretation of tongues" (1 Cor.
12:8, 10). Soon after Paul asks rhetorically, "Do
all speak with tongues? Do all interpret?" (1 Cor.
12:30). The answer obviously is no. Some do,
others do not. The same is true of all the gifts
enumerated here. This is given in the context of
the teaching about the body of Christ. Each member has his function, whether he be a hand, a foot,
an eye or an ear. Not all are hands, not all are feet.
Not all speak in tongues, not all interpret.

Some say there is a difference between "the *sign*
of tongues" and "the *gift* of tongues." They claim
that the sign is given once as the initial evidence of
the baptism of the Spirit and may never be repeated.
All Christians, they claim, must have this sign. But
the gift is something different which is given only
to certain ones, as 1 Corinthians teaches. This contention will be discussed in the next chapter.

WHERE, HOW AND WHEN IS THE GIFT OF

TONGUES TO BE USED?/ As already noted, there is a legitimate place for tongues in private use—for worship, praise and perhaps even intercession. My friends who exercise this gift tell me they are often conscious that they are interceding in prayer, although they do not know just who or what they are praying for.

In 1 Corinthians 14, Paul is also seeking to place controls on the use of tongues in the assembly of believers. When used in public, the gift is subject to certain clear restrictions. "If any speak in a tongue, let there be only two or at most three, and each in turn; and let one interpret. But if there is no one to interpret, let each of them keep silence in church and speak to himself and to God" (1 Cor. 14:27-28). Note the three regulations: Only two or three at most are to use this gift in any gathering; it must be used in turn, not in confused simultaneous speaking; there must be an interpreter present.

In the same context Paul exhorts "all things should be done decently and in order" (1 Cor. 14:40) and states that "God is not a God of confusion but of peace" (1 Cor. 14:33).

I have seen Colombian believers practice these regulations with great care. At the beginning of a prayer meeting the question is sometimes raised, "Are there any present tonight who have the gift of interpretation?" If no interpreter is present, the congregation is forbidden to pray in tongues that night.

Paul also points out that tongues may be used in private without the same regulations in force (for example, the presence of an interpreter). That is, the believer may express himself in worship, praise or intercession to God through tongues and no interpretation is necessary if he is alone in prayer.

WILL TONGUES CEASE?/ Will tongues cease? The answer to that question is yes. 1 Corinthians 13:8 says, "as for tongues, they will cease." The problem, of course, is *when.* Some outstanding Bible scholars have exegeted this passage and attempted to show, on the basis of the Greek verb for "cease" plus other factors, that tongues ceased at the end of the apostolic period. The next verses are used to prove this. "For our knowledge is imperfect and our prophecy is imperfect; but when the perfect comes, the imperfect will pass away" (1 Cor. 13:9-10). The contention is that the "perfect" refers to the written Scriptures. Thus, when the canon of Scripture was complete, tongues were done away with. The word used for "perfect" is *teleios,* which means "having attained the end or purpose, complete, perfect . . . full grown, mature . . . fully developed."[6]

Such meanings could be applied to the completed Scriptures, but the context of 1 Corinthians 13 poses a real problem for this interpretation. Paul goes on to say, "For now we see in a mirror dimly, but then face to face. Now I know in part;

then I shall understand fully, even as I have been fully understood" (13:12). When will we see "face to face"? When will we "understand fully"? Few men would dare to claim, even with completed Scriptures in hand, "I understand fully, even as I have been fully understood." Who would dare to say that he now knows as much about everything as God knows about him?

Thus, this context seems to refer clearly to the end of time, when Christ, at his coming again to earth, will bring all things to perfection, when his work through his church is complete. Then we will see him face to face. Then we will understand fully, even as he now understands us. But not before his coming will we understand fully, even with the completed Bible in hand. When he returns, tongues, prophecy and knowledge will cease, since they will no longer be necessary for the edification of the church. Until that time they are gifts given by the Spirit to build up the body of Christ.

From a practical standpoint it would border on limiting the sovereignty of God to contend that he no longer gives gifts which he gave in the early church. The reasons for tongues enumerated in 1 Corinthians 14, such as personal and corporate edification, are still valid today. If tongues are taken also as a sign to the unbelieving Jews of the apostolic period, it can be pointed out that today the same sign is needed at times. When the gospel first penetrates an area where it has never gone before,

God often seems pleased to equip his church with unusual and miraculous gifts to confirm the message. If he did this in the first century, who are we to claim that he may not choose to do the same thing again today?

It remains for us now to discuss the specific cases of tongues which are described in the book of Acts.

9

"DO ALL
SPEAK WITH
TONGUES?"

Is there a difference between "the gift of tongues" and "the sign of tongues," an outward evidence that a believer has received the baptism of the Spirit? Those who contend there is turn primarily to Mark 16:17-18 and to the three passages in Acts where tongues appear. Let's look at each of these passages.

In Mark 16, after giving the Great Commission—"Go into all the world and preach the gospel to the whole creation"—Jesus goes on to say, "And these signs will accompany those who believe: in my name they will cast out demons; they will speak in new tongues; they will pick up serpents, and if they drink any deadly thing, it will not hurt them; they will lay their hands on the sick, and they will recover" (vv. 17-18).

Many scholars hold that the "longer ending" of Mark (vv. 9-20) may have been added by someone other than Mark. However, many Christians use this as a pivotal passage to discuss the place of tongues as a "sign" in the life of a believer. Therefore, leaving the problem of textual criticism to one side, it seems necessary to discuss the implications of the content of this passage.

The contention of some is that speaking in tongues is a sign which will follow for those who believe. The interpretation is that *all* who believe *must* have this sign. The context, however, poses some knotty problems for this interpretation. *Must all* who believe also "pick up serpents"? Such a notion is the origin of the fanatical snake-handling sects of the southern U.S. But even if this were accepted (and most thinking believers will not make such a contention), what becomes of those Christians who live in an area of the world where they never see a snake? Is picking up a serpent an indispensable sign of belief? If so, those who never see snakes cannot be Christians!

Must all who believe drink poison? This would be a bizarre step which would soon decimate the church!

I have never yet met a Christian who claims that those particular signs *must* accompany *all* who believe. Yet, strangely enough, I have met many Christians who claim that the sign of tongues must accompany all who believe. To use Mark 16 as a basis for this claim is inconsistent, to put it mildly. Either we must accept all the signs mentioned there as being for all believers (including handling snakes and drinking poison), or we must accept another interpretation.

The most obvious interpretation is that the signs mentioned in Mark 16:17-18 as accompanying the preaching of the gospel are typical of the kinds of things God will do to confirm his Word. When the gospel is faithfully preached and men believe, there will be signs to authenticate this message. Some of them are the kinds of things mentioned in Mark 16. That such signs can and do appear at times is beyond dispute. That such signs always will appear for all who believe is obviously not intended.

I have seen believers in Colombia who claim this verse in protection against poisonous snakes. A zoologist once told me that all snakes in Colombia are poisonous to a greater or lesser degree. Some are lethal, others milder, but all snake bites will inject poison into the system. In the jungles and rural areas snake bites are all too common. Occasionally a believer will be bitten by a snake of such deadly poison that normally he would be expected to die. But believers will claim the power of God over that snake, rebuking it in the name of the Lord, and the person will be healed. They do not go around looking for such opportunities to prove the "signs" that follow belief. But if, in the course of their daily life, such an accident overtakes them, they will invoke this promise. God at times has been pleased to honor their faith and deliver them, just as he did to Paul on the island of Malta, as a sign to unbelievers. (See Acts 28:1-6.)

Acts is also used by some to support the contention that all must speak in tongues as a sign of the baptism of the Holy Spirit. My student friends mentioned in chapter 2 were doing precisely this. It is well to remind ourselves again that Acts was never intended to teach doctrine. It is a historical narrative of how God worked in his church at a particular time in history. What God did then illustrates what he can do now. That he will always do the same things in the same way is never suggested. That he can or may repeat the same things is perfectly true. We find in Acts some of his methods, and we can expect to see many of them repeated. But when we make the experiences of Acts normative for all Christians at all times, we leave ourselves open to the inconsistency of saying that everyone must go blind to become a Christian because this is what happened to Saul of Tarsus at his conversion. With this in mind we turn now to the passages in Acts where the gift of tongues was given.

THE DAY OF PENTECOST/
When the day of Pentecost had come, they were all together in one place. And suddenly a sound

*came from heaven like the rush of a mighty
wind, and it filled all the house where they were
sitting. And there appeared to them tongues as
of fire, distributed and resting on each one of
them. And they were all filled with the Holy
Spirit and began to speak in other tongues, as
the Spirit gave them utterance. (Acts 2:1-4)*

We have already discussed what happened at
Pentecost in terms of actual languages. The purpose was twofold. First, the gift was a sign to the
Jewish believers that Christ had now fulfilled his
promise to send the Spirit. Had there been no outward evidence, there could have been doubts about
the coming of the Spirit. Second, the gift was given
so that all men in Jerusalem that day could hear
the message of salvation in their own language and
thus understand it better.

The Jews at Pentecost, although they had believed in Christ before, were now receiving the
Spirit for the first time. After Pentecost every person who believes in Christ receives the Holy Spirit
at the moment of conversion. Paul says, "Any one
who does not have the Spirit of Christ does not
belong to him" (Rom. 8:9). Conversely, every man
who belongs to Christ has his Spirit. Thus receiving
the Spirit is not something we must wait for in the
same way that the disciples had to wait until Pentecost to receive the Spirit. He comes at the moment
of salvation. Pentecost was a historical event when
the Spirit came for the first time to form the

church, the body of Christ. Never again was the Pentecost experience repeated. Never again do we read of "a sound from heaven" or "the rush of mighty wind" or "tongues as of fire." These were phenomena that accompanied the initial coming of the Spirit and were not repeated. To make Pentecost normative for all Christians and say that all Christians must speak in tongues would mean that these phenomena should also accompany the experience. Thus, we accept the story of Pentecost as a precise description of what happened when the Spirit came for the first time. We do not make every detail of that experience normative for every Christian in all ages as part of his conversion experience.

THE HOUSEHOLD OF CORNELIUS/ In spite of the worldwide scope that Christ had given in his Great Commission ("all nations," "the whole creation," "the end of the earth"), the early Jewish Christians still did not grasp the fact that the gospel was for Gentiles as well as for Jews. God had to intervene dramatically to awaken Peter, and through him the other apostles, to this fact. God gave Peter a vision of a sheet let down from heaven and full of unclean animals which a Jew was forbidden to eat. When the voice told Peter to rise and eat, he refused on the basis of his understanding of the Old Testament Law. Then God said, "What God has cleansed, you must not call common"

(Acts 10:15).

Immediately after this vision Peter was invited to the house of Cornelius, to whom God had also spoken in a dream the day before. Peter was told by the Spirit to go "without hesitation" (10:17-20). Ordinarily Peter would not have gone to a Gentile's home, but God was forcing him out of his restricted view. Arriving at the home of Cornelius, Peter preached the gospel to Cornelius, his kinsmen and his close friends after Cornelius had explained his desire to know more of God.

As Peter was preaching "the Holy Spirit fell on all who heard the word" (10:44). Some Jewish believers who were present "were amazed, because the gift of the Holy Spirit had been poured out even on the Gentiles" (10:45). How did they know this? Because "they heard them speaking in tongues and extolling God" (10:46). Thus, the Gentiles received the Holy Spirit. Tongues were given as an outward evidence that Gentiles could also receive the Spirit. Had there been no outward evidence, Peter and the other Jews would have been hard pressed to prove what really had happened. But the gift of tongues settled the issue.

When Peter returned to Jerusalem, some Jewish believers criticized him for going to uncircumcised men and eating with them. So Peter had to defend his actions. He told about his vision of the sheet, and about how he had gone to Cornelius at his bidding, how he had preached and how the Holy

Spirit had fallen on the Gentiles in Cornelius's house. His irrefutable evidence that they had received the Spirit in the same way the Jews had received him on the day of Pentecost was that they had spoken in tongues. Therefore, no further argument could be advanced against Peter. Finally the Jews had to admit, "Then to the Gentiles also God has granted repentance unto life" (Acts 11:18). Tongues were used as the final seal of God's work through his Spirit in the Gentiles.

THE EPHESIAN DISCIPLES/

While Apollos was at Corinth, Paul passed through the upper country and came to Ephesus. There he found some disciples. And he said to them, "Did you receive the Holy Spirit when you believed?" And they said, "No, we have never even heard that there is a Holy Spirit." And he said, "Into what then were you baptized?" They said, "Into John's baptism." And Paul said, "John baptized with the baptism of repentance, telling the people to believe in the one who was to come after him, that is, Jesus." On hearing this, they were baptized in the name of the Lord Jesus. And when Paul had laid his hands upon them, the Holy Spirit came on them; and they spoke with tongues and prophesied. There were about twelve of them in all. (Acts 19:1-7)

Who were these disciples? Were they true be-

lievers before Paul came, or was their experience
incomplete due to incomplete knowledge? J. D. G.
Dunn comments,

> *Did Luke regard the twelve Ephesians as already*
> *Christians before their encounter with Paul?*
> *Their ignorance of the Holy Spirit and about*
> *Jesus, and the fact that Paul did not count their*
> *earlier baptism as sufficient but had them under-*
> *go baptism in the name of the Lord Jesus, indi-*
> *cates a negative answer.*[1]

He then develops the idea that Luke's use of the
word for "disciples" (*mathetai*) confirms that they
were not yet part of the Christian community:

> *It is true that in Acts* Mathetai *usually equals*
> *"Christians," but the 19:1 usage is unique; it is*
> *the* only *time that* mathetai *is not preceded by*
> *the definite article. Now* hoi mathetai *used abso-*
> *lutely always has the sense in Acts of the* whole
> *Christian community of the city or area referred*
> *to . . . Luke's description of the twelve as* tines
> mathetai *therefore probably implies that the*
> *twelve did* not *belong to "the disciples" in Ephe-*
> *sus—a fact confirmed by their ignorance of basic*
> *Christian matters. Indeed, I would suggest that*
> *Luke deliberately describes them in this way in*
> *order to indicate their relation, or rather, lack of*
> *relation to the church at Ephesus.*[2]

When Paul questioned them about their experience, he realized that they did not understand the
truth of the gospel. So he explained the way more

fully to them and they were baptized. "It was not that Paul accepted them as Christians with an incomplete experience; it is rather that they were not Christians at all. The absence of the Spirit indicated that they had not even begun the Christian life.[3]

They had honestly lived up to what light they had and were seeking to obey God as far as they understood his ways. But because their knowledge was deficient, they needed further explanation. When they received water baptism and the laying on of Paul's hands, the Spirit came upon them. Once again, as in the case of Cornelius, the gift of tongues accompanied their receiving the Spirit as an outward evidence that this had actually happened.

Some will take the laying on of Paul's hands as a pattern to be followed, saying that this must be done in order to receive the Spirit (or "the baptism of the Spirit," as it will often be called, erroneously, in this context). But if this is taken as normative, we immediately face the problem that it was *not* done on the day of Pentecost nor in the home of Cornelius. No one laid hands on the disciples who received the Spirit at Pentecost, and Peter had not even finished preaching when the Spirit came upon Cornelius. So it was not normative even in the book of Acts, let alone for all Christians at all times and in all places. It was Paul's way of identifying himself as a Christian with these Ephesians who were sincerely seeking the truth of Christ.

CONCLUSION/ What, then, can be concluded from these three incidents? There were certain factors common to each of these and certain differences in each one.

What they had in common was the following. First, the people involved were all devout and earnest people who were seeking God's best. Second, in no case were they specifically seeking the gift of tongues. In fact, there is no evidence that Cornelius or the Ephesians had even heard of the gift before. Thus, it was God's sovereign act which bestowed this gift. It did not come as a result of their seeking it.

What were some of the differences? On the day of Pentecost the gift of tongues was preceded by the coming of the Spirit with a sound like a rushing wind and with tongues of fire. These phenomena were not repeated elsewhere. In Cornelius's home the gift came while Peter was preaching. This is not found elsewhere. In Ephesus the gift came with the laying on of hands, an act not found in the other cases. Cornelius received the Spirit before he was baptized. The Ephesians were baptized and then received the Spirit. On the day of Pentecost the tongues were languages that spoke of "the mighty works of God." In Cornelius's case the tongues extolled God. In Ephesus the tongues were accompanied by prophecy.

Thus, even if the experiences of Acts were accepted as normative for all Christians, the problem arises as to which of the various experiences sets the pattern to be followed. It would be impossible to synthesize all these into one.

10
"THEY BELIEVED PHILIP"

Probably no New Testament passage on the receiving of the Spirit has caused more discussion and divergence of viewpoint than the case of the Samaritans in Acts 8. Because this case is unique, differing in several important aspects from the other cases we have just studied, it merits separate consideration.

Now when the apostles at Jerusalem heard that Samaria had received the word of God, they sent to them Peter and John, who came down and prayed for them that they might receive the Holy Spirit; for it had not yet fallen on any of them, but they had only been baptized in the name of the Lord Jesus. Then they laid their hands on them and they received the Holy

Spirit. Now when Simon saw that the Spirit was given through the laying on of the apostles' hands, he offered them money, saying, "Give me also this power, that any one on whom I lay my hands may receive the Holy Spirit." But Peter said to him, "Your silver perish with you, because you thought you could obtain the gift of God with money! You have neither part nor lot in this matter, for your heart is not right before God. Repent therefore of this wickedness of yours, and pray to the Lord that, if possible, the intent of your heart may be forgiven you. For I see that you are in the gall of bitterness and in the bond of iniquity." And Simon answered, "Pray for me to the Lord, that nothing of what you have said may come upon me." (Acts 8:14-24)

While there is no evidence that the Samaritans spoke in tongues when they received the Holy Spirit, some will contend that tongues must have been the outward evidence. We read in the next verse that "Simon *saw* that the Spirit was given" (v. 18). The contention is that there had to be an outward manifestation for him to see and that this must have been tongues. I would not argue against the possibility. In fact, it seems to be a fair evaluation. But it is really an argument from silence. In view of this I find myself in agreement with F. E. Bruner who says:

Tongues-speaking may indeed have occurred in

*Samaria and we have nothing against it; but
neither have we any record of it, and where a
text is silent, especially about a matter as important as the evidence of the Holy Spirit, perhaps it is best for the interpreter to remain silent
too.*[1]

THE REAL PROBLEM/ But whether tongues
were part of this experience or not, the passage is
still problematical because of another issue. The
real problem is this: Why did the Samaritans not
receive the Holy Spirit until the apostles came
from Jerusalem and laid hands on them? Some
take this as proof that the Spirit is received
through the laying on of hands, even though the
New Testament never teaches that this is necessary.
Such reasoning is generalizing from the particular.
It is using a specific case as illustrative of normative
experience. It is not exegesis of doctrinal teaching,
because there is no doctrinal teaching that says any
such thing.

But why the gap between their belief and their
receiving the Spirit? First, the situation must be
evaluated in the light of the entire biblical teaching. We have already seen that a man without the
Spirit is not a Christian (Rom. 8:9). The Samaritans had believed and been baptized (Acts 8:12).
Why had they not yet received the Spirit?

Scholars and commentators over the years have
struggled with this passage and have come up with

a variety of possible explanations. It is beyond the scope of this book to discuss all the possibilities in detail. Two interpretations commend themselves as the most probable in light of the context of Acts and the wording used.

The first can be summarized as follows. The foray into Samaria was the first major outreach of the gospel beyond Jerusalem. Reaching into Samaria was, for the Jewish believers, the crossing of a seemingly impenetrable barrier. They were moving beyond the Jewish fold into non-Jewish territory for the first time. The great gulf between Jews and Samaritans (for example, see Jn. 4:9—"Jews have no dealings with Samaritans") was being crossed, and the leading apostles themselves had to get involved. Had a church arisen in Samaria without any relation to the apostles in Jerusalem, the great rift might well have continued. The unifying work of the gospel, which makes all men one in Christ, might have been missed.

So God chose on this one occasion to do something he never did anywhere else. He made an exception to the normal Christian experience and did not allow the Samaritan believers to receive the Holy Spirit until the apostles from Jerusalem came and laid hands on them. This laying on of hands was a tangible demonstration of Christian unity. It was an act of fellowship and brotherhood which showed to all, Jews and Samaritans alike, what Paul elaborates more fully to the Ephesians:

142

*For he [Christ] is our peace, who has made us
both one, and has broken down the dividing wall
of hostility, by abolishing in his flesh the law of
commandments and ordinances, that he might
create in himself one new man in place of the
two, so making peace, and might reconcile us
both to God in one body through the cross,
thereby bringing the hostility to an end. . . . So
then you are no longer strangers and sojourners,
but you are fellow citizens with the saints and
members of the household of God, built upon
the foundation of the apostles and prophets,
Christ Jesus himself being the cornerstone, in
whom the whole structure is joined together and
grows into a holy temple in the Lord. (Eph.
2:14-21)*

The church in Samaria could not exist apart from
their fellow members of the body of Christ in Jerusalem. In order to dramatize this fact and to bring
the foundation of the apostles into clear focus,
God temporarily withheld his Spirit on this one
occasion. Never again was this necessary, since the
opening wedge had now been driven. The church
had reached beyond Jerusalem, and non-Jews were
now being received into the body of Christ. But
God chose to do this at the outset of the Christian
church, in order to highlight the unity of the Spirit
in the body.[2]

The second view is propounded by J. D. G.
Dunn in a chapter entitled "The Riddle of Sa-

maria." After explaining five ways to interpret this passage and showing how none of them solves the riddle, he proposes a completely different alternative. His contention is that the Samaritans were not yet really Christians. He gives several reasons, the most telling being the use of the verb "believe." He points out that the text does not say they believed *in* something, nor that they believed "on the Lord" (*pisteuein eis,* or *epi, kurion*). Rather it says *pisteusan tō Philippō*—"they believed Philip." Dunn says that "it signifies intellectual assent to a statement or proposition, rather than commitment to God. . . . This use of *pisteuein,* unique in Acts, can surely be no accident on Luke's part. He indicates thereby that the Samaritans' response was simply an assent of the mind to the acceptability of what Philip was saying."[3]

Dunn fortifies this point by showing that Simon, the magician, also believed and was baptized along with the rest of the Samaritans. Yet Peter pronounces a curse on him and says, "You have neither part nor lot in this matter, for your heart is not right before God" (Acts 8:21). Peter does not accept Simon as a Christian, in spite of his intellectual belief and baptism. The other Samaritans had also believed and been baptized in the same way, but had not yet received the Spirit, because it was only an intellectual belief in what Philip had said, not in the Lord himself. But when Peter and John prayed for them, they received the Spirit and became true Christians.

In contrast Dunn says of Simon,

*Simon . . . never had become a member of the
people of God. His heart was not right before
God (v. 21) but was crooked and unbelieving.
. . . Simon had not really fulfilled the conditions for the gift of the Spirit (Acts
2:38). . . . He was a Christian in outward form
only, not in the NT sense of the word. His pro-
fession and baptism mean nothing in face of the
devastating exposure by Peter. . . . What belief
he had was from start to finish centered on man
—first Philip (v. 13), then Peter (v. 24); he had
no idea of what it was to repent before God and
to put his trust in the Lord. And Luke makes it
clear (vv. 12f.) that Simon's faith and baptism
were precisely like those of the other Samaritans, as if to say, Note carefully what I say, and
do not miss the point; they all went through the
form but did not experience reality.*[4]

If this interpretation is correct (and the evidence
commends it as a sound exegesis of the passage),
the riddle of Samaria is solved. The Samaritans did
not receive the Holy Spirit at first because their
belief was intellectual and centered on Philip.
When they received a fuller understanding they became true believers and received the Spirit as all
believers do at the moment of conversion.

THE INDISPENSABLE LINK/   The two interpretations presented above are not mutually exclusive. If the Samaritans were not yet true Christians, even though they had given intellectual assent to what Philip had said, they needed to receive the Spirit and make a total commitment. God wanted to break down the wall of suspicion and enmity that existed between the Jews and the Samaritans. He wanted to demonstrate the unity which the Spirit gives to the body of Christ. So he brought the apostles from Jerusalem onto the scene to make that indispensable link. And the Samaritans became true believers under the ministry of Peter and John, which supplemented what Philip had already told them. This accords with the full teaching of the New Testament that the Spirit is received at conversion.

11
"WALK
BY THE
SPIRIT"

The hardest thing in the world is to keep balanced." This statement from L. E. Maxwell of Canada years ago became a byword among his students. It may sound like a truism, and it is, but that does not detract from its truth.

We often hear it said that Christianity is not primarily a matter of "do's and don'ts" but of "being." No one would argue with that statement. Yet it can be misleading. There are a lot of "do's and don'ts" in Christianity, and there is usually a fair balance between both the positive and the negative. In fact, whether we like it or not, the negatives sometimes outweigh the affirmatives, as, for example, in the Ten Commandments, where we find eight negative statements and two positive ones.

Few areas of the Christian life have been harder for Christians to keep balanced than the question about the person and work of the Holy Spirit. In the New Testament there are four commands related to the believer's relationship to the Holy Spirit. Two of these are negative, two affirmative. It is almost as if God is saying that in this area where balance is so hard to find he wants us to see the perfect balance.

There is no more fitting way to complete a study of the Holy Spirit in world evangelism than to look at each of these commands and ask what they mean to us as individual believers and as the corporate body of Christ. We will look first at the negative commands.

DO NOT GRIEVE THE HOLY SPIRIT/ Paul writes in Ephesians 4:30, "And do not grieve the Holy Spirit of God, in whom you were sealed for the day of redemption." Since it is possible to grieve the Holy Spirit, this implies immediately that he loves us. Sanders comments, "Grief is a love word. One can anger an enemy, but not grieve him. The words are mutually exclusive. Only one who loves can be grieved, and the deeper the love the greater the grief."[1] Every loving parent knows how true this is. The sins of our children will cause more grief than anger.

How, then, can we grieve the Holy Spirit? The

context of Ephesians 4 speaks of a whole variety of sins of word and deed. Paul refers to falsehood, anger, giving opportunity to the devil, stealing, evil talk, bitterness, wrath, clamor, slander, malice (Eph. 4:25-31). It is in the middle of this list that he exhorts us not to grieve the Spirit. Thus we see that any of these sins grieves the Spirit. Undoubtedly these verses are not intended as an exhaustive list of the only ways in which one can grieve the Spirit. Rather they illustrate how we may cause such grief. One could go on to all the sins mentioned in the New Testament and safely conclude that the Holy Spirit is grieved every time one of his loved ones sins.

We must also remember that the teaching of the New Testament on forgiveness is applicable here: "If we confess our sins, he is faithful and just, and will forgive our sins and cleanse us from all unrighteousness" (1 Jn. 1:9).

Charles Wesley, who in many of his great hymns reveals an acute awareness of his own sin, expressed this recognition as follows:

Depth of mercy! Can there be
Mercy still reserved for me?
Can my God His wrath forbear?
Me, the chief of sinners, spare?

I have long withstood His grace,
Long provoked Him to His face,
Would not hearken to His calls,
Grieved Him by a thousand falls.

149

Yet having recognized how much he had grieved the Spirit by his thousand falls, he was able to see beyond them and accept the forgiveness which Christ offered:

There for me the Savior stands;
Shows His wounds and spreads His hands,
God is love: I know, I feel;
Jesus lives, and loves me still.

DO NOT QUENCH THE SPIRIT/

The word *quench* means to put out a fire, to stifle, suppress, extinguish. The context of 1 Thessalonians 5:19 gives a clue to the meaning of quenching the Spirit. In the same breath Paul says, "Do not despise prophesying, but test everything; hold fast what is good, abstain from every form of evil" (1 Thess. 5:20-22). It is possible to quench the Spirit by despising some of the gifts which he gives. Prophecy is one of these gifts. If it is given by the Spirit and is being exercised in a scriptural way, then neither the church nor individuals should downgrade it. We have no right to make light of what God has given. Paul says we are to "test everything." But once a gift has been tested, we are not to belittle it. If we do so, we run the risk of dousing the fire which the Spirit has lighted.

Archaeologist Melvin G. Kyle once said, "We all pray for the Holy Spirit, but as soon as the tongues of flame begin to appear we all run for the fire department."[2]

A fire can also be extinguished by failing to feed it adequate fuel. If a Christian is not nurturing his spiritual life through the study of the Word of God, communication with God in prayer and obedience in his daily walk, he will soon allow the fire of the Spirit in his heart to burn low and smoulder into ashes.

On the positive side, the context speaks of things which the believer must do which, conversely, will keep him from quenching the Spirit. Some of these actions concern our relationships with others, some our relationship with God.

In our relationships with others Paul exhorts us to "respect those who labor among you and are over you in the Lord . . . to esteem them very highly in love. . . . Be at peace among yourselves . . . admonish the idle, encourage the fainthearted, help the weak, be patient with them all. See that none of you repays evil for evil, but always seek to do good to one another and to all" (1 Thess. 5:12-15). In relationship to God the exhortation is to "rejoice always, pray constantly, give thanks in all circumstances; for this is the will of God in Christ Jesus for you" (1 Thess. 5:16-18). If the believer is obeying these exhortations, he will be feeding fuel into the fire which the Holy Spirit wishes to keep alive in his heart.

One further word of caution is in order here. It is possible to quench the Spirit by scoffing at the gifts he gives. It may also be possible to quench the

Spirit by trying to work up certain gifts which he has *not* given. He gives gifts "to each one individually as he wills" (1 Cor. 12:11). But where he has not given a specific gift, one would be presumptuous to try to work up that gift or produce a fleshly imitation of it. The Spirit does not need our help to impart a gift. All he asks is our grateful acceptance of what he gives.

We turn now to the two commands which are *positive* exhortations to the believer about his relationship to the Holy Spirit.

WALK BY THE SPIRIT/ The first command is in Galatians 5:16: "But I say, walk by the Spirit, and do not gratify the desires of the flesh." Once again the context of the command concerns interpersonal relationships between Christians. Listen to Paul as he leads up to this important command.

For you were called to freedom, brethren; only do not use your freedom as an opportunity for the flesh, but through love be servants of one another. For the whole law is fulfilled in one word, "You shall love your neighbor as yourself." But if you bite and devour one another take heed that you are not consumed by one another. (Gal. 5:13-15)

Thus, walking by the Spirit will involve loving my neighbor. If I am not loving my neighbor, I am not walking by the Spirit.

One of the most Spirit-filled men I have ever

known is Victor Landero. He has shown the fullness of the Spirit through his gifts, in the fruit of
his life and in his daily walk. This fullness has often
been manifested in his relationship to his neighbor.

One time he and I were sharing together in a
Bible conference ministry in the backwoods of
Colombia. One evening he told me quietly that he
would not be around the following day until late in
the evening. When I asked why, he explained that
one of his brothers had a big job to complete that
day on his farm, and Victor had offered to help
with it. I discovered that the farm was located over
nine miles away. Victor planned to rise early in the
morning, walk nine miles through the woods,
spend the day helping his brother with his crop,
then walk nine miles back to join us at the conference. And that is exactly what he did!

The next night he was back in time for the evening service, having walked a round trip of eighteen
miles and worked the better part of the day in hard
farm labor. All this work was simply to help
another man whom he loved. That type of love is a
far better demonstration of walking in the Spirit
than many more spectacular things which might
attract more attention.

The relationship to God also forms part of the
context. As Paul exhorts the Galatians to walk by
the Spirit, he goes on to describe the works of the
flesh which are at war with the Spirit: "immoral-
ity, impurity, licentiousness, idolatry, sorcery,

enmity, strife, jealousy, anger, selfishness, dissension, party spirit, envy, drunkenness, carousing, and the like" (Gal. 5:19-21). By contrast Paul describes the fruit of the Spirit as "love, joy, peace, patience, kindness, goodness, faithfulness, gentleness, self-control" (Gal. 5:22).

Anyone who lives or works among students today knows that there are few things young people are seeking more than the first three of these fruits of the Spirit. Whether they be Christian or non-Christian, the youth of today are calling for love, joy and peace. How many posters on university campuses are extolling the merits of love (however that word may be defined by those using it)? How many of today's songs call plaintively for a return to the lost joy of another age, or reflect a wistful reaching out to joy in some form in the future? How many demonstration marches have called for peace, with the peace symbol prominently displayed and the peace sign held high? Even though the definition of the words may not be biblically based in the thinking of those using them, there is, nevertheless, an almost universal call which represents a deep longing to see these fruits manifest in daily life. The tragedy is that many who use the words do not know the only One who can give them their true significance.

Inter-Varsity Christian Fellowship holds an annual Overseas Training Camp in Latin America. At the third annual camp in Guatemala some of

our students went on an out-trip which required
walking long distances into mountainous territory
where Indians lived. One of the students lost his
sleeping bag along the way. This was serious, since
it was cold in the mountains.

Two or three days later an Indian Christian
caught up with the students on the trail and presented the fellow with his lost sleeping bag. The
Indian had found the bag and had *walked twenty-
one hours* through rugged terrain to return it! This
was motivated by Christian love for a brother in
need and was a true manifestation of walking by
the Spirit and demonstrating the fruit of love.

BE FILLED WITH THE SPIRIT/   The final command to be considered is found in Ephesians 5:18:
"And do not get drunk with wine, for that is de-
bauchery; but be filled with the Spirit." In order to
understand it one must see the whole context in
which it is written. Paul goes on to say that Christians should be "addressing one another in psalms
and hymns and spiritual songs, singing and making
melody to the Lord with all your heart, always and
for everything giving thanks in the name of our
Lord Jesus Christ to God the Father. Be subject to
one another out of reverence for Christ" (Eph.
5:19-21).

The finest exposition of this passage I have read
is by the Reverend John R. W. Stott. I gladly
acknowledge my indebtedness to him for a fuller

understanding of this portion of Scripture. Much of what I say here will reflect the exegesis found in his outstanding book, *The Baptism and Fullness of the Holy Spirit.* In fact, I found his book so helpful that I arranged to have it published in Spanish in order to share his insights with Latin brethren, who were experiencing many of the gifts and much of the fullness of the Spirit, and who needed to understand these things better in the light of Scripture. Several personal conversations with John Stott on this and related topics have also been helpful to me.

We turn, then, to consider this command.

THE NATURE OF THE COMMAND/ Three things must be said about the command "be filled with the Spirit." First, it is plural, indicating it is for all Christians. No Christian is left without the need for the infilling power of the Spirit of God. This is to be a universal experience, the norm for all Christians, in distinction to the gifts of the Spirit, which are divided up among believers, with no one gift being the indispensable norm for all to possess.

Second, the command is in the passive voice. The New English Bible translates Ephesians 5:18, "Let the Holy Spirit fill you." Thus, the filling is not something the individual can work up for himself. It depends on the intervention of the Spirit. Stott wisely points out, "Nevertheless, it must not be imagined that we are purely passive agents in receiving the Spirit's fullness, any more than in getting drunk. A man gets drunk by drinking; we become filled with the Spirit by drinking too, as we have already seen from our Lord's teaching in John 7:37."[3]

Third, the command is in the present tense. One of the simple lessons a first-year student of Greek learns is that the aorist tense represents a one-time action, while the present tense represents a continuous action. This is especially true of the imperative. An aorist imperative commands that an action be done once and for all. A present imperative commands that the action be continued. Thus the verb here can be translated, "Keep on being filled with the Spirit." It is significant that this verb is present and not aorist. Were it aorist the implication would be that the fullness of the Spirit is a one-time action that never needs to be repeated. Once filled, the believer would always remain full. But the use of the present tense shows just the opposite. This fullness is something which the believer needs to have continually renewed in his life.

This truth is borne out in the book of Acts, as already noted in chapter 3. It is clear in Acts that the same individuals are repeatedly filled with the Spirit, even though they received the initial filling on the day of Pentecost or at the moment of conversion.

THE RESULTS OF THE COMMAND/ When a man is filled with the Holy Spirit, several things result. Paul describes them in graphic terms.

First, a Spirit-filled man gains self-control. The fullness of the Spirit is set in contrast to the drunkenness of the body. The man who is filled with the spirits of alcohol loses control of his physical and mental faculties. By contrast, the man who is filled with the Spirit of God gains self-control by giving control to the Spirit. One of the fruits of the Spirit is specifically mentioned as "self-control" (Gal. 5:23). Thus a man does not lose control of himself but rather gains a sanctified, God-given control. This is demonstrated in the development of a healthy and happy relationship with God and other people, as seen in the statements below.

Second, the fullness of the Spirit results in fellowship with other Christians. Paul says Christians should be "addressing one another in psalms and hymns and spiritual songs," an expression of brotherly love similar to that which will characterize walking by the Spirit. The first of the fruits of the Spirit is love. If we are filled with the Spirit, we will love our brothers. If we love our brothers, we will want to communicate with them. Stott says that "we cannot claim the fullness of the Spirit if we are not on speaking terms with any of our fellows."[4] Yet how often have we seen Christians who claim to have the fullness of the Spirit (perhaps because of some outward manifestation) yet whose relationships with other Christians leave much to be desired?

Third, the fullness of the Spirit results in worship, as seen in the phrases "singing and making melody to the Lord with all your heart, always and for everything giving thanks in the name of our Lord Jesus Christ to God the Father." True Christianity has always been a singing Christianity. It has been said that the Reformation sang its way into the hearts of men. Martin Luther composed some of the great hymns which we still sing today, such as "A Mighty Fortress Is Our God" and "Away in a Manger." When men come into a right relationship to God and are filled with the Spirit, a natural result is to sing. Giving thanks to God will accompany this.

In Colombia one of the characteristics of the church, when the believers were manifesting a genuine fullness of the Spirit, was that they all prayed out loud together in prayer meetings. This was not an uncontrolled confusion but rather an audible expression of praise and worship from all who were present. One of the side benefits I discovered in such prayer meetings was to be able to listen to what others around me were praying about. It struck me again and again that much of their prayer time was spent in praise and thanks to God. Instead of jumping into petitions which centered on themselves or their own needs, they usually spent the majority of their time thanking and praising God for who he is and what he has done.

Fourth, the fullness of the Spirit results in submitting to one another. "Be subject to one another out of reverence for Christ." The verb here is not in the imperative but rather is in participle form, making it parallel to the preceding participles— "addressing," "singing" and "giving thanks." In this case the Authorized Version rather than the RSV gives the more correct sense by translating it "submitting yourselves one to another in the fear of God." "Not self-assertion but self-submission, is the hallmark of the Spirit-filled Christian," says Stott.[5]

Thus the primary results of the filling of the Spirit are worship to God and fellowship with other Christians. Although Paul does not specifically make the point in this passage, it is well to remember what we have seen in Acts, as studied in chapter 3: In every case where Christians were filled with the Spirit, the immediate result was a sharing of their faith, a proclamation of the gospel in one form or another. If, when we are filled with the Spirit, we desire to speak to each other and to God, it is safe to assume that there will be a similar desire to speak to others who do not know God.

Victor Landero told me of a time in his life when he had no opportunity to witness to non-Christians for a period of six days. "Imagine!" he exclaimed. "Six whole days without speaking to

one person about Christ! I thought I would burst!"
Nothing less than the fullness of the Spirit could
have produced that kind of feeling. Witnessing to
others is not natural or easy, but it will result from
the fullness of the Spirit.

OBEYING THE COMMAND/ The next logical
question one may ask is, "How can I be filled with
the Spirit?" Two things need to be said in response.

First, there are times when the fullness of the
Spirit comes as a sovereign intervention of God in
the life of the believer, not as a result of that person's special seeking. This is seen in most of the
nine cases in Acts where believers were filled with
the Spirit. In few, if any, of those cases were the
individuals specifically seeking the fullness of the
Spirit at the moment they received it. Yet God
gave it to them, knowing they needed it to face a
particular crisis or to fulfill a particular task.

Having said that, we must note, secondly, that a
command would not be given unless there were
some way for believers to obey it. So there will be
many times when the fullness of the Spirit will be
the result of conscious, definite effort on the part
of the Christian. Volumes have been written on
this topic throughout the history of the church.
Some are complicated and involved. Others are
simple and clear. It is not within the scope of this
book to go into great detail here, but it may help

to give just three observations that seem to sum up the general tenor of Scripture on this important doctrine.

I once heard Hans Burki of Switzerland say, "To be filled with the Spirit is to be filled with the Word." The more I have thought about that, the more true it seems to me to be. If a man wants to be filled with the Spirit, he must saturate himself with that which God has revealed about himself and his plan for us. This information is found in the written Word of God.

In addition to the Word, prayer becomes a vital link in our relationship to God. God speaks to us through the Word; we respond to him in prayer. The person who neglects prayer can scarcely be in a position to obey the command to "be filled with the Spirit." Fellowship with God is a vital part of this fullness.

Finally, obedience to what God says to us through his Word and through prayer is equally important. God has revealed in his Word all that we need to know to live a godly, Spirit-filled life. But if we disobey that Word, we cannot expect the fullness of the Spirit. By contrast, the believer who conscientiously obeys all that he understands of God's Word for his own life will be a Spirit-filled Christian.

One of the most obvious characteristics of my friends in Colombia who were so evidently filled with the Spirit was their absolutely unswerving obedience to what they found in the Bible. No questions were asked. If the Bible said it, it must be obeyed. The simplicity of their faith in obedience was beautiful to behold, and it was the key to the fullness of the Spirit in their lives.

In summary, if we are to obey this command, we can do so through filling our life with God's Word, communing with him in prayer and obeying him in our daily walk.

EPILOGUE

During the preparations for Urbana 73 (Inter-Varsity's tenth missionary convention) many of us were again impressed with the leading of the Holy Spirit in the lives of the believers, especially as it relates to world evangelism. One session we felt essential for Urbana 73 was a major address on "Evangelism and Social Concern." What is the relationship between those two things? Are they one and the same? Are they mutually exclusive? Or are they two sides of the same coin? Can we evangelize without having a concern for the social needs around us?

As we prayed about and discussed who should be invited to bring this key address, we considered numerous people who seemed qualified theologically, academically and in other ways. But somehow we could come to no firm agreement on who among the various possibilities was God's man for the job.

One day in our planning committee meeting someone stressed the need to get a person who would not talk from a theoretical, "ivory tower" position, but one who knew what he was speaking about on the basis of grassroots experience. We should invite someone who had a record of deeds done in the fields of both evangelism and social concern. That night as I contemplated this suggestion, it dawned on me that perhaps we were starting from the wrong angle. We had been looking for a person with academic and theological qualifications, when we should have been looking for someone personally involved in evangelism and in meeting the social needs of people around him.

Suddenly the name of Gregorio Landero came to mind. Gregorio, a farmer in Colombia, was led to Christ by his brother Victor. Although he had never had the opportunity to go to school (not even to first grade, let alone high school, college or seminary), Gregorio had learned to read and had saturated himself with the Scriptures. With his brother, he had begun an aggressive outreach of evangelism and church planting, so that today there are dozens of churches and hundreds of believers spread over a vast area in northern Colombia as a direct result of his witness.

In the course of his work with the churches Gregorio became heavily burdened for the acute problems of poverty which surrounded him on every side. Such conditions took their constant toll on the lives of his fellow citizens and greatly affected the development of the church. Gregorio determined to do something about this. Over a period of several years he studied the Scriptures on this point, interacted with fellow believers, consulted government and university agencies, and did everything within his power to find ways to help poverty-stricken Colombians to a better life.

The result was the establishment of *Accion Unida* (United Action), a program of social outreach concerned with improving agricultural methods, home hygiene, medical facilities, dental help, literacy programs, vocational training and anything else that would meet the total needs of men. Interwoven in the entire warp and woof of the program, and underlying all they did, was direct evangelism—the presentation of the claims of Jesus Christ as the only Savior of men.

So why not ask Gregorio to speak at Urbana 73 and tell in a practical way how God is at work in a specific situation in one area of the world? I consulted our planning committee and received enthusiastic agreement that this was what we should do.

The next step was to contact Gregorio. To do so by mail would be difficult. How could I explain to him in an adequate way what Inter-Varsity is all about, what Urbana 73 was, and exactly what we wanted him to do? Personal contact seemed the only solution. So in the summer of 1972, in connection with another trip, I was able to arrange a last-minute, hurried visit to Colombia.

Gregorio met me in Cartagena, where we spent two days together. Not having seen each other in several years, yet having been the closest of friends, it was a delightful reunion. First, he shared with me how God had led him in the development of *Accion Unida.* Then I explained to him what Inter-Varsity Christian Fellowship is and what role the Urbana convention plays in the purposes of the movement. I outlined for him the program of Urbana 73 and explained the crucial role of the message on "Evangelism and Social Concern."

Then I said, "Gregorio, we believe you are the man God wants us to invite to address the convention on this topic."

He was utterly overwhelmed with the invitation. The idea that he, a farmer from the backwoods of Colombia, whose only formal schooling was some Bible institute studies, should address 15,000 university students in the United States was more than he could grasp. He dropped his head in his hands and wept silently for several moments. Then we prayed together. Finally, he said he could not give me an answer until he had opportunity to discuss this with Victor, whom he considered his spiritual father as well as his brother, and to pray seriously about it.

The next day Gregorio, in a quiet, unassuming way, said to me, "You know, I believe God has been preparing me for this invitation. A month ago Victor told me that God had revealed to him that very soon I was to receive an important invitation to minister in something big, and I was not to turn it down."

It also came out the next day that a month prior to my visit to Colombia someone in the remote village of Corozalito had prayed in tongues. An interpretation was given, and it proved to be a prayer for me and my forthcoming trip to Colombia. That was several weeks before I had even thought of going to Colombia!

A third factor also came to light. At about the same time of the prayer in Corozalito (which coincided closely in time with Victor's word to Gregorio), someone in the Buen Pastor Church in Cartagena, which my family and I had attended for nine years, had also prayed in tongues. The interpretation was a prayer for a Colombian who very soon was to be invited to minister in the United States, that God would prepare him for this ministry.

All three of these things happened independently of each other and before the idea of going to Colombia to invite Gregorio had even come to my mind. But for the Colombians they all seemed a very normal part of life.

Yes, the Spirit of God is still at work. He has his

unique and wonderful ways of leading us into all truth. Our task is to walk in the Spirit day by day in the light of the written Word of God.

NOTES

Chapter 1

1. *In some cases throughout this book numerous other Scripture references are available but just a representative passage is given.*

Chapter 2

1. *John R. W. Stott,* The Baptism and Fullness of the Holy Spirit *(Downers Grove, Ill.: InterVarsity Press, 1964), pp. 22-23.*

Chapter 4

1. *Harry R. Boer,* Pentecost and Missions *(Grand Rapids: Eerdmans, 1961), p. 47.*

Chapter 5

1. *Monsen II, quoted in George Meri Haddad,* Aspects of Social Life in Antioch in the Hellenistic Roman Period *(Chicago: University of Chicago Thesis, 1949), p. 128.*

Chapter 6

1. *Lesslie Newbigin,* The Household of God *(New York: Friendship Press, 1954), p. 171.*
2. *Ibid., pp. 173-74.*

Chapter 7

1. *Oswald Sanders,* The Holy Spirit and His Gifts *(Grand Rapids: Zondervan, 1970), p. 110.*

2. *Donald Gee,* Spiritual Gifts in the Work of the Ministry Today *(Los Angeles: L.I.F.E. Bible College Alumni Association, 1963),* see Table of Contents.

3. *Frederick Dale Bruner,* A Theology of the Holy Spirit *(Grand Rapids: Eerdmans, 1970), pp. 138-39.*

4. *W. F. Arndt and F. W. Gingrich,* A Greek-English Lexicon of the New Testament *(Chicago: University of Chicago Press, 1957).*

5. *Ibid.*

6. *Gee,* Spiritual Gifts, *pp. 94-95.*

Chapter 8
1. *One example of this position is found in William J. Samarin,* Tongues of Men and Angels *(New York: Macmillan, 1972).*

2. *Bruner,* A Theology of the Holy Spirit, *pp. 282-83.*

3. *Sanders,* The Holy Spirit and His Gifts, *p. 125.*

4. *Ibid.*

5. *Gee,* Spiritual Gifts, *p. 68.*

6. *Arndt and Gingrich.*

Chapter 9
1. *James D. G. Dunn,* Baptism in the Holy Spirit *(Naperville, Ill.: Alec R. Allenson, 1970), p. 83.*

2. *Ibid.*

3. *Ibid.*

Chapter 10
1. *Bruner,* A Theology of the Holy Spirit, *p. 179.*

2. *See Bruner for a more detailed exegesis of this view.*

3. *Dunn,* Baptism in the Holy Spirit, *p. 65.*

4. *Ibid.*

Chapter 11
1. *Sanders,* The Holy Spirit and His Gifts, *p. 92.*

2. *Quoted by Addison Leitch in* Interpreting Basic Theology *(Great Neck, N. Y.: Channel Press, 1961), p. 125.*

3. *John R. W. Stott,* The Baptism and Fullness of the Holy Spirit, *p. 47.*

4. *Ibid., p. 43.*

5. *Ibid., p. 45-46.*